SERIES EDITOR

Cinema is a fragile medium. Many of the great classic films of the past now exist, if at all, in damaged or incomplete prints. Concerned about the deterioration in the physical state of our film heritage, the National Film Archive, a Division of the British Film Institute, has compiled a list of 360 key films in the history of the cinema. The long-term goal of the Archive is to build a collection of perfect showprints of these films, which will then be screened regularly at the Museum of the Moving Image in London in a year-round repertory.

BFI Publishing has now commissioned a series of books to stand alongside these titles. Authors, including film critics and scholars, film-makers, novelists, historians and those distinguished in the arts, have been invited to write on a film of their choice, drawn from the Archive's list. Each volume will present the author's own insights into the chosen film, together with a brief production history and a detailed filmography, notes and bibliography. The numerous illustrations have been specially made from the Archive's own prints.

With new titles published each year, the BFI Film Classics series will rapidly grow into an authoritative and highly readable guide to the great films of world cinema.

Annie Girardot as Nadia

ROCCO
AND HIS BROTHERS
(ROCCO E I SUOI FRATELLI)

. . . .

BFI PUBLISHING

First published in 1992 by the
BRITISH FILM INSTITUTE
21 Stephen Street, London W1P 1PL

British Library Cataloguing in Publication Data

Rohdie, Sam
    Rocco and His Brothers
    I. Title
    791.4372

        ISBN 0–85170–340–2

            Designed by
Andrew Barron & Collis Clements Associates

            Typesetting by
Fakenham Photosetting Limited, Norfolk

        Printed in Great Britain by
    The Trinity Press, Worcester

CONTENTS
· ·

For Rebecca

ACKNOWLEDGMENTS

I would like to thank Ed Buscombe, Roland Caputo, Roslyn Glickfield, Ann Langusch, Julie Marshall, Geoffrey Nowell-Smith, Beverley Purnell, Bill Routt, Richard Thompson, David Wilson. Markku Salmi checked the credits.

Luchino Visconti on the set of *Rocco and His Brothers*

INTRODUCTION

. . . .

Rocco and His Brothers is the story of the Parondi family, who come to Milan from the poor Italian South to try to make a new life for themselves in the industrial North. The father has died before the film opens. The first scene is the arrival of the Parondi at Milan railway station: Rosaria, the mother, with Simone, Rocco, Ciro, Luca; the eldest brother, Vincenzo, is already in Milan, and at the moment the family arrives he is celebrating his engagement to Ginetta, also from a family of southern migrants.

The film centres on the disintegration of the family and its traditional values in modern urban Italy as represented by Milan. The source of this disintegration is less economic than emotional-erotic. Each of the brothers attempts in a different way to come to terms with Milan. Simone, the second eldest, becomes a boxer but is led astray by an obsessive passion for the prostitute Nadia.

Nadia rejects Simone, and he falls apart. His career goes downhill and he becomes, over time, dissolute and desperate, taking to petty theft, homosexual prostitution, gambling and finally murder. Rocco, the next eldest, good and pure, tries to save Simone, thinking he will thereby save the family. Nadia and Rocco fall in love, and when Simone finds out he rapes Nadia in front of Rocco and the two brothers fight each other into senselessness.

Rocco, hating boxing, becomes a boxer to help pay off Simone's thefts; after the rape, he gives up Nadia, for the sake of Simone's lost honour. Nadia rejects Simone with disgust, and in a fit of rage and hurt Simone murders her. Once again, Rocco tries to shield Simone for the sake of the family and his ideals of brotherly love, but Ciro, a worker with Alfa-Romeo, gives Simone up to the police.

The eldest brother, Vincenzo, like Ciro, seeks family interests in personal success and integration in the economy of the North. It is Rocco, most attached to the peasant values of the South and most committed to maintaining them, who ends by compromising them, becoming the instrument for the destruction of the family, not the guardian who protects it – not for lack of will, but rather by the inappropriateness of his gestures. The traditional world to which he clings has no relevance in the modern world in which he lives. Notions of honour, the family, solidarity, transposed to Milan, become the source not of good, but of an uncontrollable descent into evil.

It is left to the youngest brother, Luca, to bring together the industrial North and the rural South, worker and peasant, in a vision of a unified Italy at once human and progressive – though less as real possibility than as ideal hope.

The force of the film is not in these messages, but in the melodramatic actions which effectively deny them, not with ideological hopes, but with excessive, passionate despair. The centre of things is with Simone and Rocco, not the workers, Vincenzo and Ciro, nor with Luca, the symbolic figure of social-ideological unity. The film is divided between a political ideology of progress and a decadent human reality beneath its surface. However doomed that reality, it is the one to which Visconti, like Rocco, is most attached.

I
....

Visconti sketched out the idea for *Rocco and His Brothers* (*Rocco e i suoi fratelli*) in spring 1958 for the producer Franco Cristaldi. He worked on a treatment with Vasco Pratolini, the novelist, and Suso Cecchi D'Amico, his preferred scriptwriter, who had collaborated with him on *Senso* (1954) and would work on virtually all of Visconti's subsequent films. The treatment was ready that summer, but Visconti and Cristaldi had some disagreements and the project eventually went to the producer Goffredo Lombardo at Titanus. Pratolini withdrew and the script was worked on by five writers (including Visconti), each of whom wrote one of the five 'chapters' around which the film is structured: Massimo Franciosa ('Vincenzo'), Suso Cecchi D'Amico ('Simone'), Pasquale Festa Campanile ('Rocco'), Enrico Medioli ('Ciro'), and Visconti himself (the final chapter, 'Luca'). Visconti used the same group of writers for *Il gattopardo* (*The Leopard*, 1963), and later singly for other films.

Each 'chapter' took the name of one of the five Parondi brothers in order of age from the eldest to the youngest. The script assumed its final form by autumn 1959. Shooting began in Milan on 22 February 1960, and was completed on 2 June 1960 at Civitavecchia.

Though the film is wholly set in Milan, some scenes had to be shot elsewhere, notably, and controversially, the scene of the murder of Nadia by Simone at the Milan flying-boat station. The provincial authorities refused Visconti permission to use the station, afraid that a scene involving murder and prostitution would be bad for tourist development in the area; it was shot at Lake Fogliano in Latina instead. For most other film-makers the change in location, to simulate one reality with another reality, would hardly have mattered; but for Visconti, whose realism is fastidiously authentic, the shift to Lake Fogliano was a reluctant compromise. In the event, this setback proved the least of subsequent censorship difficulties the film was to face, and the further compromises Visconti was forced to make.

The credits list a collection of short stories, *Il ponte della Ghisolfa*, by the Milan writer Giovanni Testori, as having inspired the film. (In the year *Rocco* was released, Visconti staged Testori's *L'Arialda*, and in 1967 his *La monaca di Monza* [*The Nun of Monza*]). The most important stories for *Rocco* in the collection are the trilogy *Il ponte della Ghisolfa* (*Ghisolfa Bridge*), *I ricordi e i rimorsi* (*Memories and Regrets*), and *Un letto, una stanza ... (A Bed, a Room ...*), which are about a love affair of a woman with her husband's brother. The story is told from her point of view; one of the best passages is her meticulously detailed revulsion for her husband as he comes to bed, drunk and smelly, and her image of the more delectable brother, which makes the reality of her husband so intolerable. In *Rocco*, the differences between Rocco and Simone, joined over Nadia, find part of their symbolic charge in a physical contrast: the fresh, sweet beauty of Rocco (Alain Delon) and the shambling, unshaven, mean, desperate Simone (Renato Salvatori), with the appearance but also the stink of decadence.

A similar situation of incestuous passion, more closely related to *Rocco* because of its setting among Italian immigrants in Brooklyn, is Arthur Miller's play *A View from the Bridge*, which Visconti directed for the theatre in 1958 at the time he was thinking about *Rocco*. (Visconti also directed Miller's *Death of a Salesman* in 1949, *The Crucible* in 1955, and *After the Fall* in 1965.) The play involves not only incest and 'brotherly' jealousy, but traditional Southern Italian 'honour' put at risk in a modern urban setting, close to what occurs in *Rocco*.

Other literary sources for the film were important during the writing of the script: Thomas Mann's *Joseph and His Brothers* and Dostoevsky's *The Idiot*. Mann and Dostoevsky (like Testori and Miller) were particularly favoured by Visconti. His 1971 film *Morte a Venezia* and his 1956 ballet production *Mario e il Mago* (*Mario and the Magician*) were based on Mann stories; in 1946, Visconti staged an adaptation by Gaston Baty of Dostoevsky's *Crime and Punishment*; and he adapted the Dostoevsky story *White Nights* for the film of the same name (*Le notti bianche*, 1957).

The Mann novel has a definite presence in *Rocco*. The novel, like the film, juxtaposes mythic, primal forces and historical, social ones; and it concerns, as *Rocco* does, the confrontation of different worlds and moralities, which in the film are an industrial Italian North and a primitive rural South. Visconti, like Mann, was fascinated by disintegrating worlds, values in crisis, the historicity of relations, for which, in both novel and film, the family is the historical and psychic centre.

The character of Rocco is directly based on Dostoevsky's Prince Myshkin in *The Idiot*, the pure innocent in a corrupt world whose Goodness ends by provoking Evil. It is joined to other Dostoevskian themes of guilt, remorse, sacrifice. The link between a moral universe and a social-historical one, the crisis in the one felt in the other, is characteristic of Visconti (and also of Mann), and more generally of a realistic-melodramatic literature of the late nineteenth century whose best Italian expression was not in letters but in lyric opera, particularly the operas of Giuseppe Verdi.

II

....

Besides the Testori stories, there are three Italian sources for *Rocco*: Giovanni Verga's 'veristic' novel *I Malavoglia*, Antonio Gramsci's fragmentary essay 'The Southern Question', and, overall, the operas of Giuseppe Verdi.

The juxtaposition – Verga and Gramsci, the novel and social analysis – is at the heart of *Rocco*, and is central to Visconti's other purely literary choices, works which construct circles of relations between private and public, the fictional and the historical, family and society. Verga and Gramsci have an extra, specific importance for *Rocco*, a film about the experience of Southern Italian immigrants coming from the poor rural South to the developed Italian North: 'I've always seen the Southern question as one of the principal sources of my inspiration,' he said in 1960.[1]

The 'Southern Question' in Italian politics has been a question of economic difference, class exploitation, political deals, but also involves the shape of Italian culture, the cultural price of development, the destruction of traditional relations by capitalist ones. The film is a product of that culture, not simply representing the 'Southern Question' but representative of it.

The post-war Italian 'economic miracle' altered not only traditional peasant cultures, but also a traditional elite bourgeois culture, which was Visconti's own and whose forms and values structure the film. The film is encased within a cultural history as much as the Parondi family are enmeshed in a social one. The forms of the film belong to a bourgeois culture as threatened by modernity as is the peasant culture which those forms in the film are used to represent. The events which occur in the fiction have a mirror in the shape of the fiction itself.

The fictional story of *Rocco* concerns the dislocation of traditional values of a peasant culture transplanted into an industrial one. The historicity of those values, their inevitable displacement, is not simply a matter of fiction but a matter of history. In the space of just over a decade, from the mid-1950s to the late 1960s, Italy was transformed from a relatively backward agricultural economy to an advanced capitalist one. For the depressed South, the miraculous economic development of Italy was socially and culturally traumatic. The South became a symbol of an entire Italian experience of economic change and social disruption.

One aspect of the Italian literary and filmic reflection on the South was regret and nostalgia for values lost, a humanity and warmth forever gone, destroyed by neo-capitalism and its neo-bourgeoisie. It is *the* theme and obsession, for example, in the works of Pasolini even when the Italian South shifts to India, to a mythical Arabia, to the Yemen, to Morocco where Pasolini sought in the peasant third world what had ceased to exist for him in Calabria or Basilicata, or in the slums of Naples or the shanty towns of the Rome *borgate*. For intellectuals like Visconti and Pasolini, the cultural loss caused by economic development affected them not because the South had disappeared, but because their own cultural values, the humanism they had learned and valued, seemed also on the verge of disappearance, as culturally moribund as the Italian Southern peasantry was historically irrelevant. Unable to adjust fully to the modern, these film-makers, each in their way, made films which involved a regret for the loss of the past. By 1960 (the year of *Rocco*), when Pasolini made his first film, *Accattone*, juxtaposing the 'human' values of a sub-proletarian world (a symbolic South) with the inhuman new bourgeois universe surrounding it, the third world, peasant civilisation image of the South had become, by the very force of change, abstract if not absurd.

Nostalgia for a past destroyed could appear politically radical and socialist since there was in that nostalgia an admixture of anti-bourgeois, anti-capitalist feelings. It connected to a Marxism and a loyalty to the Italian Communist Party by film-makers like Visconti, Pasolini and Giuseppe De Santis which was often sentimental and sometimes reactionary, for example when it became a rejection of the modern in all its manifestations, especially of the avant-garde, of new artistic forms, condemned not on artistic grounds but for a lack of apparent (or obvious) political value.

Rocco, Simone, Rosaria in *Rocco* are victims of the new modern North into which they are plunged, but they are also the heroic figures of the film, especially in their defeat. They may have lost their worlds but, for the fiction, the loss ennobles them. Their grandeur is in their victimisation: purer, better values destroyed by vulgar, instrumental, lesser ones.

It isn't simply the theme of that regret *in* the fiction of *Rocco* that matters, but the means for structuring it, a last-century classical humanist culture: Verga, Mann, Dostoevsky, Verdian opera, melodrama, the historical novel, Chekhov, Shakespeare. The centre of *Rocco* may be the defeated peasant world, but the staging of that defeat implicates a defeated old bourgeois world. The film depicts, with an obsessive realism, the history of what is already past at the moment it is being represented, and in fictional forms of the past.

Rocco is a film whose artistic and narrative structures belong to a culture which predates the cinema and for which the means of cinema are used to revalue and at the same time make present again as attesting to the historicity of those values. *Rocco* is not a modern work (because of the classical forms it uses), but a contemporary one (for the consciousness of its own history). Visconti measured all that has been lost, the price of an inevitable, unwelcome progress, in a meticulous nostalgia; it is the exquisite detail of his measure that makes his work at once current (for its politics and history) and remote (for its forms and culture).

In the case of Pasolini, the consciousness of loss, often taken to the point of absurdity, nevertheless employed singularly modern terms to express a thoroughly unmodern nostalgia and regret. Visconti, who in many ways was more modern than Pasolini in his politics and in his acceptance of economic and social changes (as *Rocco* attests), was more old-fashioned in the forms he clung to (as *Rocco* also attests). While Pasolini parodied or cited classical culture, from Chaucer to Mannerist painting, the forms of that culture are the very texture of Visconti's films – like *Rocco*, a nineteenth-century melodrama more to do with Verdi, than with, say, Minnelli or Douglas Sirk.

At the level of ideology *Rocco* is progressive, but its structures and language seem not to be, or at least that is the problem Visconti's film poses: is there any relevance now to the forms of operatic melodrama and the historical novel, as lovingly, as accurately reproduced in *Rocco* as are the streets and bars of Milan, or the bruises to Simone's face, or the tearing of flesh by a knife? And is there in these forms and in the culture and values they represent something more productive than a lament and nostalgia? Can those values not only point to values lost, but to values to be regained?

III

Of the five Parondi brothers, Vincenzo, the eldest, and Ciro and Luca, the two youngest, are integrated into the industrial society of the North. Vincenzo has a secure construction job, Ciro is a skilled worker for Alfa Romeo, and the family hopes that Luca will return to Lucania in the South, to the village which the family had left, but a village being transformed by economic progress within a more prosperous South. The fate of the three 'integrated' brothers directly refers to ideological and social-historical positions argued by Gramsci in 'The Southern Question'.

Gramsci saw the Southern question of North–South disunity in class terms. He regarded the relation of the industrial North to the rural South as one of exploitation by a political bloc of Northern industrialists and large, semi-feudal Southern landowners. Rather than workers in the North taking the Southern peasantry as their natural allies against the bourgeois state, and rather than Southern bourgeois intellectuals regarding the peasantry of the South as their allies, the working class aligned itself with Northern capital, while Southern intellectuals detached themselves from solidarity with the Southern peasantry to attach themselves instead to the national bourgeoisie of the North and its promise of a share for these intellectuals in a national and European culture.

Gramsci called for an alliance, under the leadership of the Communist Party, between the Northern working classes and the Southern peasantry against the exploitative relations of capital and its political manifestations in the state. Land reform in the South – the break-up of large estates and the redistribution of land to an essentially landless peasantry – was impossible, he argued, so long as Southern landowners protected their privileges and property relations by political support for Northern industrialists. Exploitation in the South of the peasantry and exploitation in the North of the working class were, according to Gramsci, part of the same structure of economic and political relations. The remedy for Southern backwardness, and for national disunity, and a national economic progress which would be more evenly and equitably shared between regions and classes, could only occur, Gramsci reasoned, by means of an anti-capitalist, anti-bourgeois class alliance between workers and peasants against the bourgeois state, a 'class' state, neither 'national' nor 'popular'.

Social class, Gramsci argued, held the key to genuine development and real political unity. Ciro, the worker at Alfa Romeo, and Luca, who would return to the South, are part of the Gramscian progressist ideology which the film adopted. Ciro, by becoming a conscious member of the working class, and Luca, by being assigned a position in a new-order South, are given essentially social roles by the film. They are made to represent social-economic choices politically wider (and hence politically more valuable) than private, individual interests.

The emphasis with regard to these three brothers, especially Ciro and Luca, is on consciousness, choice, rationality, understanding, social commitment. All this is very worthy, but the trouble is that however fine the ideological positions of Ciro and Luca may be, their dramatic positions are weak and their characters are without substance. While Visconti clearly approved of the good worker Ciro at Alfa Romeo, it was the defeated in the film, whose choices were individual, passionate and out of step with the socially useful, who tempted his attentions and focused the film's energy. The ideological weight of the film is with Ciro and Luca, but its dramatic force is with Simone and Rocco, the victims of the ideology represented by their more socially progressive and integrated brothers. It is as if the film is divided between its

Production still: Max Cartier as Ciro

ideological commitment (which is artistically dull) and its artistic commitment (which is politically retrograde).

The dramatically interesting Simone and Rocco – interesting for their passion, their individuality, their traditional values of honour, family, sacrifice, their excess, in short their humanity – may be criticised (and victimised) for an ideological lack, but the ideologically interesting brothers seem to lack all humanity (they betray their own brother). Not only does Vincenzo desert his family and refuse to help Simone, and Ciro hand Simone over to the cops, but these acts of 'betrayal', of lack of solidarity, of unconcern for the family, are measured by their lack of dramatic depth as characters. They seem mere shadows to the 'substance' of Rocco and Simone, as if they are made of cardboard. In the historical-ideological universe of the film the shadows may be important, but in its fictional, dramatic universe they are of little real account.

The ideology of the film, despite appearances, is not in the progressist Gramscian positions of Ciro and Luca, but in the retrograde ones of Rocco and Simone. They may lose, they may be defeated, but their defeat is a testament to the human vacuity of the progress which defeats them. The film is not on the side of its ideological heroes, but on the side of its passionate and more fictionalised heroes, those who, like the film itself, have been formed by a past whose importance is asserted while their inevitable demise is recognised. It is as if in the world gained by Ciro and Luca there is nothing left of any importance, while in the world lost by Simone and Rocco there is everything of value, including the aesthetic energy which has created it.

The radical force of Visconti is in his attachment to the past in protest against the culture and values wrought by the present. It is a politics and art of nostalgia registering the irrevocable nature of its own passing, like the Prince of Salina in *The Leopard*, all alone in the streets at dawn, contemplating his own death and contemporary irrelevance after the tastelessness of the ball in a world become vulgarly bourgeois.

IV

By 1960, when *Rocco* was released, not only was Visconti's culture which had structured the film being rendered obsolete, so too was its progressist ideology. The ideological weakness of *Rocco* has to do as much with the inadequacy of that ideology to encompass the economic and social reality of Italy as with the cardboard characters of Luca and Ciro.

As early as the late 1950s, Gramsci's class alliance of Northern workers, Southern peasants and committed intellectuals, under the guidance of the Italian Communist Party, as the answer to the 'Southern Question', had been overtaken by events. The Party had underestimated the power and flexibility of Italian capital and had overestimated the political determination of Italian workers, and perhaps as well its own capacities.

There had already been a vast migration of Italian peasants to Northern industrial cities, while investment by private capital and by the state in the South had become significant. It was no longer possible to maintain the image of Northern exploitation of a poor South, or, given the degree of economic integration and development, of a radical North–South division. Politically, Italian social democracy was able to contain radical socialist demands as the liberal wing of the ruling Christian Democrats initiated a measure of social reform and was soon to join with the Socialists in an anti-Communist centre-left coalition to give Italy centrist, democratic, relatively stable and moderately reformist governments.

The 'progressive' anti-capitalist class alliances hinted at in *Rocco* and explicit in Gramsci had little force by 1960 as bourgeois social democracy proved itself attractive, not only to conservative groups, but also to socialists and to the working class. In any case, it was not only Visconti's nostalgia for a past which vitiated the progressive ideology of *Rocco*. The progressive ideology itself was a product of a nostalgia; and both together part of a world on the wane.

V
....

If Ciro and Luca are the ideological characters of the film, as if lifted whole from the pages of Gramsci, Rocco and Simone are the more fictionalised characters, who come from the pages of Thomas Mann, Dostoevsky, Testori and Arthur Miller, but principally, in so far as the film concerns Italy and the South, from Verga and his *I Malavoglia*, published in 1881.

I Malavoglia was the direct literary source for Visconti's second feature, *La terra trema* (1948), the narrative of a Sicilian fishing family trying to end the exploitation of the fish wholesalers in the village by setting out on their own, only to be defeated by natural and economic circumstances. At the end of *La terra trema*, the members of the family leave the village which can no longer economically sustain them for work in 'the North'.

Rocco was initially conceived as a sequel to *La terra trema* (despite the more than ten-year gap between the films) and as part of a larger trilogy. (Visconti imagined Ciro becoming an established, successful bourgeois, indeed a 'grand bourgeois'. Perhaps for that reason it might be permissible to think of his *La caduta degli dei* [*The Damned*, 1969], with its story of the decadence of a high bourgeois family, albeit German and under Nazism, as the third film of the trilogy.) In the script for *Rocco*, the story begins in Lucania with the burial of the father at sea by the brothers; not, as in the film, with the arrival of the family at Milan railway station. The images in the script of the sea, the burial, the departure, directly link with the closing shots of *La terra trema*.

Visconti's great heroic figures dream of going beyond themselves: Gino in *Ossessione* (1942), 'Ntoni in *La terra trema*, Maddalena in *Bellissima* (1951), the Contessa in *Senso*, King Ludwig in *Ludwig* (1973) and Tullio in *L'innocente* (1976). In *Rocco*, the principal dreamer is Rosaria, who brings her sons to Milan to make good and who imbues them with her dream. Inevitably, dreams – always dreams of a freedom, and often, as in *Rocco*, lower middle-class dreams of economic success ('People call me signora now,' Rosaria writes to Rocco over images of her being greeted by the sugary smiles of shopkeepers) – turn sour and destroy the dreamer in the face of the hardness of the reality which the dreams were first dreamt to overcome.

It is in the passion of the dream, and the energy expended for its realisation, that the full force of the reality to be met, and the full disaster in not meeting it, are realised. If, it can be argued (and Visconti so did), the essential conflict of *Rocco* is economic and social, the power of the film lies in the dream to go beyond the limitations imposed by the social; and to that degree, to the degree it touches those limitations and boundaries, it indicates their power. It is not the social and economic which succumb to dreams in *Rocco*, rather it is the dreamers who are defeated by the solidity of a reality they only completely accept in being crushed by it.

In that sense the dream – or, to shift things slightly, fiction – is the very means for understanding reality, for seeing it in the first place. The split in the film between the fictionally flat Ciro and Luca, who are nevertheless historically and ideologically dense, and the fictionally dense Simone and Rocco, who seem so anachronistic as to demonstrate only their own historicity, require each other as the counterpoint between reality and the necessary detour through dream and fiction in order to know it.

The scenes of discovery by Visconti's heroic victims of how illusory are their dreams and how unforgiving is reality are among the most dramatic moments of his films. They are the place where the melodrama of the form, the histrionics of acting and gesture as part of that form, and the historical reality which defeats all attempts to refashion it, come together, where the strength of fiction and the power of reality finally meet.

In *Rocco* – and the entire film has been orchestrated to this scene – that meeting occurs when Simone rings the doorbell of the Parondi home during Rocco's victory celebration and reveals, to the accompaniment of the most extreme hysteria, that he has murdered Nadia. The whole force of the film, and the main point of an extensive, rhythmic, musical montage of cross-cutting (almost from the beginning of the film) between Rocco and Simone, between dreams and their impossibility, find their climax at this moment: all the sacrifices by Rocco have had no avail, all the solidarity he fought for, all the renunciations he experienced have not only not helped Simone or the family, but contributed to their final ruin: 'Adesso, è finita.' ('It's all finished.')

It is at this place of melodramatic extremity that the politics of *Rocco* are effected in the realisation of the impossibility of passions to overcome History and power and yet the contrary realisation of the human necessity of seeking to do so. What ennobles Rocco and Simone is their damnation. What damns Ciro, and especially Vincenzo, is their mediocrity, their willingness to conform, their bland acceptance of what Rocco and Simone so passionately refuse. And the means for comprehending this contrast is in melodrama; that is, in a form whose content is the quality of excess of the form and whose function is to offer an understanding of a historical real world which penalises that excess (and all that is human in it) and rewards its absence.

Melodrama, by theatricalising reality, reveals it while at the same time revealing the impossibility, the unlivability of the emotions it calls up, except within melodrama – that is, not in life but in art. The overheated fiction of melodrama becomes simultaneously revelation of the real, protest against it, and salvation from it, the place where the values denied by reality, or defeated by reality, can still survive. This is less a political faith than a refined aesthetic one where politics seems to enter as an alibi.

'Their final ruin': Simone and Rocco after the murder

VI

The divisions – flat characters/dramatic characters, social/individual, ideology/fiction, present/past – correspond to others which divide the film, and have divided its critics. These divisions involve a contrast in *Rocco* between a realism of detail and an artificiality of performance, as if the film were split between document and melodrama, cinema and theatre, the prosaic and the extraordinary, the historical and the psychic. And, even if the weight of the film rests on the side of the second set of terms (the dramatic and the fictional), that weight, however unbalanced, is only measurable in contrast with the first set (the ideological and the social). Rocco and Simone, for example, only make sense in relation to Ciro and Luca.

What gives *Rocco* much of its force, and beauty, is that the structural divisions are also thematic, and though a case can be made for the incompatibility of its progressive ideology and its nostalgic forms, in fact the aesthetic at work in *Rocco* makes no distinction between form and content. The realistic details, for example, are both setting for the drama and dramatic in themselves, decor *and* meaning, fact *and* significance. The lavish detail of objects, furniture, clothes, streamers, balloons, cakes, facial expressions at Vincenzo's engagement party has exceptional dramatic and symbolic weight as contrast to the 'isolation' and 'poverty' of the Parondi family arriving at Milan station and Vincenzo's failure to meet them. It is also a contrast to their arrival at his party, which threatens, then destroys, its gaiety. The details are not merely realistic and authentic but dramatic and theatrical. The 'drama' of the scene is as much in the decor of the party and its musical chatter, suddenly silenced by the ringing of the doorbell, as in the sharp reversal of mood when Rosaria and her sons enter the Gianelli household.

The asymmetry of terms between ideology and fiction or document and melodrama, and the greater force of the latter, is not a defect or even a weighting of one value against the other, but a sign of the inadequacy of reality to render up its truth; hence the overweighting of the drama, of the melodramatic gesture, of the histrionic performance as signifiers of a depth of repressed passions and inexpressible feelings. Melodrama is the means for making reality speak, for making history come alive, for giving ideology its 'human', psychic sense.

The excess of feelings is signified in the film, not by language, but by gesture, or by grunts, screams, gnashing of teeth, well beyond the prosaic reality being presented. Even the most banal detail seems overcharged. And, with Verdian opera as a model, whole scenes can become orchestrated sounds (the arrival at Milan station) or characters give vent to performances akin to operatic outbursts: the 'duets' between Rosaria and Nadia, the 'choruses' at Vincenzo's engagement party, the neighbourhood chorus at Rocco's victory celebration, Cecchi's two wonderful arias, and the boxing sequences where emotions are immediately translated into spectacle and the spectacle is the sight and sound of blows, thuds, shouts, pain, a theatre of boxing as the only place the 'inarticulate' Rocco can express his torment.

As in opera, articulation in *Rocco* is extraordinary, as if deep emotion can only find expression in the inflated gesture which bursts through a surface realism and yet is also contained by it. In the ordinary way, the most fictionalised and dramatic characters in *Rocco* are the least articulate, but it is they, not Ciro (the mouthpiece of progressive ideology) or Luca (its symbolic hope), who box, who shout, who groan, who fight, who murder, who rape, who suffer and gesticulate, whose instinctual and physical sounds become music, and who are defeated by those not given to such extravagance, like the untuneful, 'flat' Ciro.

The structural divisions in the film are part of an argument, or rather of an aesthetic which needs to justify its spectacle by reference to the unspectacular. The 'dramatic' is seen to be directly caused by the repressive order of society. It is this repression that gives rise to Simone's violence, to Rocco's sacrifice, to Rosaria's hysteria. There is always in *Rocco* a 'real' historical-political and social reason for theatrical artifice and dramatic excess. Rocco's generous impulses and Simone's delinquent ones, and the defeat they suffer as a result, take their force in relation to a world which has become alienated and ordinary. Rocco and Simone may be 'anachronistic', but the historicity of their actions becomes so much more 'human' in acting against a history, against the modern world, against the present and the everyday. Not only do they burst the bounds of the ordinary, but a lesson is being read by the film of the ordinary as repressive; hence to go beyond it is not only to appear exceptional and rare, like the operatic

'diva', and like her to engage in extraordinary expression, it is also to strain against the forces which necessitate that expression. The diva bursting into song, or Simone into an inarticulate rage, come from the same impulse of seeking a depth beyond the normal and finding an extraordinary means for uttering it.

Visconti insisted that the defeat of his heroes was always a social defeat caused by the organisation of society, and it was that order, even including its forms of expression, which the extravagant gestures of the characters in the fictional world of *Rocco* directly challenge, and which the film itself challenges in the melodramatic extravagance of its forms.

VII
. . . .

A challenge to the order of society through artistic forms was, if not a commonplace by the early 1960s, certainly a common practice by an avant-garde claiming that experiments with language and structure, beyond the conventional, had social and political significance. The critique of that avant-garde position, especially from sections of the political left, was that the connection between formal innovation and political commitment was at best tenuous and at worst non-existent. For example, much of the criticism levelled at the films of Antonioni was of this kind, namely that there was no precise social understanding for the plight of his characters, nor even a clear realistic motive, and hence his experiments with narrative form, dramatic structure, the shape of character, not to mention shadow, light and graphic design, seemed to lack any social and therefore any political rationale. His characters appeared to be not only socially desituated but, like their narratives, inexplicable.

The areas of experimentation in Antonioni's films were visual and dramatic. Both the images he created and their narrative sense were constructed as uncertain and ultimately unknowable, without clear sense, or centre; they were changeable, tenuous, fragile, evanescent, not the things on which political faiths could easily be built. If it could be argued that the conventional language of politics was a language of certitudes, the language of Antonioni's films was precisely the reverse of that, a language which decertified, dedramatised, decentred. Political language itself was being challenged, or, for those who could see it, a new political language was being offered.

Where Antonioni was reticent with explanations, though expansive in his formal innovations, Visconti was profuse with reasons and declared motives for the fictional events of his films, while conservative in his means. Visconti's formal excess derived from novelistic and operatic structures whose principal virtue was in an overemphasis of explication, a persistent marking and nonstop underlining. Visconti's inarticulate characters, like Rocco and Simone, never cease making noise or waving their arms about to emphasise the ineffability of their feelings, while the film underscores such gesticulations with its own emphatic gestures, for example a parallel 'dramatic' montage setting one emotion against another, one mood against its reverse, narrative structures of hysteria matched by the hysteria of the action being portrayed, as in the 'classic' montage of Nadia's murder and Rocco's boxing match which comes from melodramatic film conventions (the chase, the last-minute rescue) and the melodrama of lyric opera (the sequence is like the finale of Bizet's *Carmen*, which intercuts Escamillo fighting the bull with José murdering Carmen).

In relation to the narrative innovations of Antonioni, which owed a debt to the best of the tendencies in Italian neo-realist films toward de-dramatisation and 'objectivity', Visconti moved in the opposite direction, and not only in technique, but in time, back into the past. His rationale, quite independently of the social and cultural nostalgia which justified his stepping backward, was that his way was politically correct, that by reading out social-political lessons, by providing a social context for actions and a social commentary on actions taken, it avoided an 'asocial', 'formalist' aesthetic. The 'melodramatic' was an explicative and therefore political framework. The artifice of theatre was thus seen as the most effective means for the revelation of reality. For Visconti, reality unexplicated in the manner of Antonioni (and in part also of Rossellini) was reality without political sense or purpose and hence socially without value. The more 'worthy' political credentials of Visconti were contained in his choice of the overcharged artistic form of melodrama, and thus, in another and quite unexpected way, his form was a content.

VIII

Nadia's murder by Simone is very beautiful yet horrible, meticulously staged yet sensuous, symbolically rich but so palpable that the feel of the knife piercing Nadia's flesh can be precisely measured; her writhings, however artificial, are delicious, however posed, excruciatingly real. What is true of the murder is true of the rape, of Rocco and Simone's fight, and of all the staged fights in the boxing ring, emblematic in the film of the theatricalisation of reality, the turning of everything into extraordinary, artificial spectacle.

What is incredible about the surface realism of *Rocco* is its lavishness, so extreme, fastidious and detailed as to be swamped by the effort of its rendition (could anything be that detailed?); so finely wrought and profuse that it passes almost directly from the real to the artificial. Visconti's reality always seems abstract and studied, the art of the casual rather than the fact of the casual (as in Antonioni). In the effort to present the real, it is the artfulness of the presentation that is most noticeable. The reason for this, at least in part, is that the real is meant in his films to signify, and not what lies on the surface of reality but what seethes beneath it. To make reality speak required, it seems, considerable effort.

Because reality is pointedly significant and dramatic in *Rocco*, it loses specificity as object or person, to attain to a generality of meaning and to the typicality of history. The Parondi family is not this specific family but representative of all Southern families, of an entire Southern experience (more than nine million Southern Italians made the journey to the North between 1955 and 1971), of a whole culture (hence their dress, their comportment, are always socially emblematic); not this family, but all families like them, not this arrival in Milan but all arrivals of the same kind, not this coat, this button, this meal, but this coat, button, meal as a sign of the socially typical. Little history and big History are indissolubly linked in the studiousness of *Rocco*'s details. To make History real, Visconti particularises it; to give the particularity significance, it is recycled into the general. All events, all things tend toward the sample specimen, and hence toward social abstraction.

Actions and object, at once precise and exemplary, attain to the exemplary by the accuracy with which they are rendered, yet the rendering, which turns reality into an artefact and a thing of beauty, is at the same time its theatricalisation, its making-of-it-noticeable, an art of detail in which detail becomes spectacle. The making of all things artistic can transform the most sordid reality into a thing of beauty. The rape scene is something quite sublime in *Rocco*, as torture and sadism are not in Pasolini's *Salò*.

Art helps then to clarify reality and endow it with significance, while also saving reality by beautifying it. Art becomes in this manner not only value, but refuge. It addresses the world but is also the means to escape it as one might flee to a book or a painting in a vulgar world. Visconti, a committed political artist, in the very act of underlining political meanings in his fictions, came close to affirming a faith in art against contemporary reality. In Life, one might prefer Ciro, but in Art, Simone was far more preferable, far more tempting. And it is in Simone (and Rocco, Rosaria and Nadia) that all the artistry of the film is concentrated, whereas Ciro, part of the political and historical universe of the film, the wave of the progressive contemporary future, is given short artistic shrift.

Visconti's aestheticism went beyond, I think, the formalism and decorative emptiness with which Antonioni was sometimes charged.

'An art of detail in which detail becomes spectacle'

Could it really be argued that an escape into Art and Beauty as enduring values with which to accuse the present was an advanced progressive politics?

IX
....

It is at first sight very odd to have Visconti's aestheticism and theatricalisation of reality (and History) applauded by substantial segments of the cultural left, as it was by *Cinema Nuovo* and its editor, Guido Aristarco. *Rocco* was praised for its political correctness, more correct for *Cinema Nuovo* than the 'naturalism' of neo-realism, and certainly more correct than the dedramatised, unstressed narratives of Antonioni. In the case of neo-realism, and of Antonioni, the 'objectivity' and the lack of stress failed not only because no clear political lesson was being drawn, but because it implied an acceptance of the world rather than an analysis of it and/or a demand for its transformation which, *Cinema Nuovo* argued, was the very sense of Visconti's melodramatic and theatrical highlighting. Visconti's attitude toward reality, the journal asserted, was critical, *hence* theatrical; the attitude of the neo-realists toward reality was instead accepting, *hence* naturalistic. It was as if the sign of Visconti's political realism lay in his artistic excess, and the more excessive it was, the more politically pointed it could be. What Visconti possessed, Aristarco argued, was the documentary naturalism of neo-realism, to which he added a critical dimension whose forms derived from the theatre and the novel; that is, reality *and* culture, naturalism *and* consciousness, the former from the present day, the latter from the past.

In an article on *Rocco*, Aristarco pointed to the Verdian operatic passages in the film, the 'arias', 'duets', 'choruses' which interrupted the ordinary logic and naturalistic action in order to isolate and put in 'close-up' really significant relations and meanings. Such 'cultural', 'artistic' intervention in the real, forcing it to signify, was a means, according to Aristarco, to bring significance to History; that is – and this goes back to the theatricalisation of detail and to the profuse lavishness of the settings – it is a way to shift the concrete toward the general, the particular toward the typical. Thus at the very moment that objects lose their particularity, they enter History and the exemplary. And not only do the objects in the film make this entrance, the entire film does so as exemplification of History and as political lesson.

'Rocco,' Aristarco wrote, 'is not a tragedy. It would be so if it had expressed itself within the context of decadent literature. Visconti relies instead on actions of diverse and opposed human destinies and elevates these to *the height of the typical*, which, by the contrast between negative and positive positions, illuminate the essential problems of an "Italian history"'[2] (my emphasis). Art, to this left culture, was essentially a political instrument. And, in the moralism of the left of the late 1950s, Visconti, despite all appearances to the contrary in his films, argued similarly, and especially so for *Rocco*.

The film criticism of *Cinema Nuovo* (the cultural influence was Lukács, the political one, Gramsci) took the decadent cultural aspects of Visconti and turned them to political account, not as decadence, but as political statement and historical criticism. In effect, what it regarded as politically radical and responsible found its cultural artistic correspondence in what was part of a high bourgeois culture of the past, thus linking, as Visconti had linked in practice, progressive political culture with a traditional artistic one supported by a moralism which condemned the artistic avant-garde and what was modern in the cinema as political and social evasion, as lack of 'commitment'.

X

The 'Rocco' chapter begins with Rocco coming out of the barracks at Civitavecchia where he has been doing his military service. He goes out along a dockside to read a letter from his mother telling him news of the family: that Vincenzo is married, that Ciro is working for Alfa Romeo, and that the shopkeepers call her 'Signora'. In effect the letter describes the family as settled, beginning to be prosperous, becoming integrated into the rhythms of Milan. Rosaria ends the letter by asking Rocco to send her some money. He finishes reading it, goes to the telegraph office, and sends his pay home.

The letter is not simply read but represented in scenes from Vincenzo's life, of Ciro on the factory floor, of Rosaria being smiled at in shops. The scenes have no temporal specificity. They signify a frequent occurrence, and are meant to suggest the 'typical'.

Outside the telegraph office Rocco bumps into Nadia, who has also been in Civitavecchia doing 'service' for the past fourteen months, in prison for prostitution. They take off round the town in a horse and carriage (she pays), have a coffee at a table outside a café (she pays), and find themselves suddenly attracted. It is the beginning of a romance whose mood is soft, genuine, lyrical. The meeting, the coffee, their touching hands are accompanied by the music on the soundtrack with which the film began and which enters periodically, a 'destiny' theme, transposed by Nino Rota from the opening of Tchaikovsky's Fourth Symphony. It has two 'moods' in the film, one of dramatic foreboding, the other lyrical and romantic, both of which are sounded at the Rocco–Nadia meeting.

These moods in the scene are also moods related to time. The lyricism and the romance belong to something present, whereas the doom and foreboding belong to a future which suggests that the present of the romance may be doomed (and all the more precious for having no future). There is also a temporal asymmetry in the meeting. Given Nadia's profession (prostitution), the meeting with the saintly, even 'aristocratic' Rocco is a kind of redemption through love. The sense of their exchange (she gives money rather than takes money) is different from her exchange with Simone (who takes money to give to her), whom she 'tempts' into theft and crime to 'afford' her. But the meeting has come 'too late' to save Nadia, and in fact rather than saving her, the meeting with Rocco dooms her to rape, and death.

The sadness of the scene is a sadness related to time which literally overwhelms the characters and the film. Rocco, Simone, Rosaria, in so far as they are victims of a History which they are out-of-step with, are victims of time: they are anachronistic, coming 'too late', as the romance between Nadia and Rocco comes too late to save her, or to save Rocco, or Simone, or the happiness of the family. Enmeshed in the drama and tragedy of these four anachronistic figures are eternal values and feelings of honour, of blood, of solidarity, which seem to predate History itself or to belong to an epoch before the progressive force of time had any influence.

The theme of anachronism, being out-of-step with History, is figured in the film by repeated scenes of 'bad timing', of things coming too early or too late as if emotions and actions were not synchronised with the movement of time any more than they are with the settings of things in space.[3]

There is a quality to *Rocco* which often gives greater force to decor than to the actions which occur within it. Objects take on psychological and dramatic qualities, oppressing characters, even expelling them, in an expulsion so extreme that characters burst into histrionic movements and inflated gestures as if their surroundings had kept down their emotions. Just as there is a gap in time between what they feel and what the 'times' can bear, so too is there a gap in space or context, between what they need to express and the space permitted for that expression; hence the bursting in and out of spaces, which is not a mere theatricality of exits and entrances but spatial explosions, the lid coming off. The most violent, dramatic exchanges between characters occur in overcrowded spaces, weighed down by decor and objects as a weight of things and of History, from nylon stockings to balloons.

'Bad timing' is a constant in *Rocco*. It is realised in a variety of ways, most interestingly when the film directly works on time itself, the dramatic highpoint of which is the cross-cutting between Rocco's boxing match and the murder of Nadia by Simone. The cross-cutting occurs elsewhere in the film, sometimes – as in the 'Rocco' chapter – in blocs of contrasts which build to the hysterical finale of the boxing match and murder. The form is familiar from the codes of silent cinema, certainly in place by the time of Griffith.

As in the finale of *Rocco*, this form consists of cross-cutting events which are simultaneous in fictional time but represented as successive on the screen, in such a way that time is dramatised (by contrasts) and spatialised. Distinct fictional spaces are understood as temporally simultaneous and yet far enough away spatially as to risk, as in the last-minute rescue, coming 'too late'. The anxiety, the excitement, the hysteria of the last-minute rescue is in the possibility, spatially realised in the parallel cutting, that the two separate spaces – but simultaneous times – will *not* join up and that the girl will be violated, or the train will sever her limbs, or the Indians will pillage and burn, in any case that the hero will arrive too late. It is a fear, in part, of being irrelevant, obsolete, anachronistic. And, given the obsolescence decreed by time to the

Art Center College

dramatic characters of *Rocco*, their victimisation by History and the historicity of their emotions, that they arrive too late and are, like anachronisms, too late in their very being, this highly codified technique of the cinema, codified perfectly for the emotional high temperature of popular film melodramas of the 1920s, is equally perfect for *Rocco*. Like those melodramas, it is a theatre of the hysteria of the 'too late'.

The cross-cutting of the boxing match and the murder is at the end of the 'Ciro' chapter, the consequences of which spill over into the final 'Luca' chapter. The construction, though perhaps already prepared in the very first scenes of the film, is mainly worked out in the preceding 'Rocco' chapter, beginning with the fateful meeting of Nadia and Rocco at Civitavecchia. But then it is organised not as cross-cutting of simultaneous times but rather as contrasts of events in a progressive linear time.

The sequence of events in the 'Rocco' chapter is roughly as follows: meeting of Nadia and Rocco at Civitavecchia; sparring in the gym between Rocco and Simone (with the sense that Rocco has already 'displaced' Simone in boxing as he has displaced him in love); Rocco meets Nadia at the tram stop and they embrace (the romantic displacement); Simone is beaten in the ring (professional displacement); Simone's friend, Ivo, tells Simone of the love affair between Nadia and Rocco (confirmation of the one displacement in the context of the other); the rape of Nadia by Simone in front of Rocco (revenge for the romance); the fight between Rocco and Simone (revenge for the loss of the boxing career); Rocco rejects Nadia and tells her to return to Simone (an attempt to return to the past – 'too late'); Nadia returns to Simone (too late) in despair and hatred; Rocco wins a boxing match (as a symmetrical close to the loss of a match earlier by Simone).

The contrasting scenes between the linked fates of the two brothers over boxing and Nadia are also linked by matters of decor, which brings the film back to a time in the first chapter after Simone has won his first fight and just prior to his love affair with Nadia, when the boxing promoter Morini comments on the violet colour of Simone's boxing shorts, 'the colour of champs and vamps', echoed later in the film during the rape scene, when Simone flings Nadia's knickers in

Simone confronts Rocco and Nadia, he rapes Nadia and flings her knickers in Rocco's face

Rocco's face. These contrasts, in progressive linear time, continue through most of the 'Ciro' chapter until the finale, which is composed in a 'classical' cross-cutting of simultaneous times successively represented, leading in this case towards not one but two climaxes, first the murder, then the revelation of it during Rocco's victory celebration.

The importance of what immediately precedes the cross-cutting, and further ties Simone and Rocco, is in Rocco's agreement to pay off Morini for the money Simone stole from him (to be able to 'afford' Nadia) which forces Rocco into a career in boxing which he doesn't like or want. Boxing is his 'sacrifice' for Simone, his attempt to redeem him and save the family.

The cross-cutting is organised as follows:

Preparation: The lights go up in the stadium for the boxing match; Rocco is in his dressing room/Simone is in a bar and learns that Nadia is prostituting herself at the Milan flying-boat station.

First Encounter: Rocco and his opponent eye each other as their gloves are fitted/Simone spies on Nadia at the flying-boat station.

Round One: Simone tries to 'cover' Nadia with her coat and she runs away/Rocco is badly shaken in the ring and Cecchi, his trainer, tells him to 'cover' himself/Simone pulls a knife and advances towards Nadia.

Round Two: The two fighters close and Rocco knocks his opponent down/Simone repeatedly stabs a screaming, writhing Nadia until she dies and he runs off.

Final Round: Rocco wins.

The cross-cutting is not the familiar one from chases and last-minute rescues in the American cinema. In *Rocco* there is a parallelism between events which makes the murder of Nadia 'like' the defeat of Rocco's opponent. Even words and gestures are exchanged between the vast space and distance between events. Cecchi's words to Rocco are responded to by Simone (he covers Nadia). Simone's blows at Nadia are echoed in the blows by Rocco in the ring.

The 'tragedy' of the scene is contained in its sense of bad timing. As Rocco tries to save Simone, Simone is destroying himself by the murder of Nadia in a symmetrically opposite and simultaneous action. It is too late and futile, the one parallel but opposite action dooming the other which was meant to save it, as if the fates of the brothers are so linked that the linkage is expressed not only in a montage of time but in

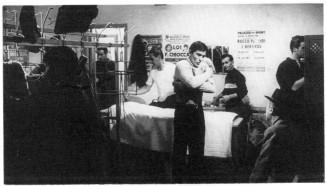

Cross-cutting between the boxing match and the murder.
Top: The lights go up in the stadium. *Middle:* Rocco in his dressing room. *Bottom:* Simone
learns that Nadia is prostituting herself

Top: Rocco and his opponent eye each other
Middle: Simone spies on Nadia at the flying-boat station
Bottom: Simone tries to cover Nadia with her coat

Top: Rocco is shaken in the ring
Middle: Simone pulls a knife and advances on Nadia
Bottom: Rocco knocks his opponent down

Top: Simone repeatedly stabs Nadia
Middle: He runs off
Bottom: Rocco wins the fight

a transfer of gestures; it is Rocco, and not simply Simone, who is murdering Nadia (true symbolically and emotionally, and also visually), and it is Simone, and not simply Rocco, who is winning in the ring. Isn't the fight a fight to save Simone? Isn't Rocco's victory his victory?

The anachronism, historically, of Simone and Rocco, which gives their futile actions a political/cultural force, is echoed by events in the fiction of actions coming too late, being anachronistic and out of synchronisation with the temporality of other actions by other characters. The force of the scene of the murder/boxing match, and its hysteria, comes from the sense of how close the two parallel actions are, and at the same time how hopelessly distant. And while History is being echoed by fictional time, fictional time has been shaped by a structure of simultaneity and succession as a signifier of a temporal gap which can never be closed. It is a structure of two things closely aligned symbolically, indeed direct analogies, but which can't be brought together in the 'facts' of the 'reality' represented by the fiction. Time completely defeats Simone and Rocco, but the film, in the analogy it invents to represent that defeat, overcomes the corrosive, terrible power of time. The film synchronises (as a filmic structure) what it represents as out of synchronisation within the fiction. Simone and Rocco may be anachronistic, and Rocco's actions come 'too late', but what is out of step in the space of the fictional world can be placed side by side in the film, compared, cross-cut, made into analogies, as if the film by means of its art had conquered the time which defeated its characters.

The sadness of what time does in the story of *Rocco* (it destroys lives) is counterpointed by the victory over it by the film's impulse toward analogy as a means for regaining through beauty and poetic symbol what has been lost through time. This is the precise point at which the aestheticism of the film is a taking of sides against the progress whose inexorability it so carefully details (the defeat of Simone/the victory of Ciro). In that sense the unmodernity, the turning to sources and forms which historical time had culturally consigned to the past, was a protest by means of a cultural history against History itself for the sake of a notion (and practice) of art which, however culturally bound, is nevertheless presented as having transcended those boundaries.

XI

....

From 1953 to 1973 Visconti staged twenty-one lyric opera productions, principally at La Scala but also at Covent Garden and Spoleto. Most of the operas were *melodramma italiano* of the nineteenth century, works by Puccini, Bellini, Donizetti, Spontini and above all Verdi. 'My choice of the lyric repertoire is dictated by my taste for melodrama: and it is Verdi whom I most prefer and who offers the possibility of a total spectacle where everything is expressed in a perfect theatrical aesthetic.'[4] Ten of the twenty-one operas he staged were by Verdi: *Macbeth, Falstaff, Simon Boccanegra, Il trovatore* (twice), *Don Carlo* (twice), *La traviata* (three times).

In the early 1950s opera repertoires shifted towards nineteenth-century opera, which was a move away from purely musical values in opera towards an integration of music with dramatic values carried by words, dance, settings and acting as much as by music and voice. Visconti was a symptom (and a cause) of the overall shift toward 'dramatic' opera and staging, best expressed by *melodramma italiano*, but which also included the works of Gluck and Strauss, which Visconti staged (*Salome, Der Rosenkavalier, Ifigenia in Tauride*), and of Wagner, which he did not.

Stage directors like Visconti became very important for opera in the 1950s, also the period of divas like Maria Callas, who was theatrically accomplished and could dramatically carry the gestures and histrionics of Italian 'Grand Opera'.

Visconti helped to create Callas. He used her in his first five productions (*La vestale, La sonnambula, La traviata, Anna Bolena, Ifigenia in Tauride*), shaping her to his conception of Italian melodrama. 'Above all the character of the "diva" fascinates me, this extraordinary being whose place in the theatre needs to be re-evaluated. In modern myth the diva is the incarnation of all that is rare, extravagant and exceptional.'[5] Rosaria is the 'diva' of *Rocco* as Maddalena is of *Bellissima* and Livia Serpieri of *Senso*, all works, like the Verdi operas in which Callas starred, that are *melodramma italiano*. Visconti wanted Katina Paxinou to play Rosaria precisely because her acting style was so emphatic and 'melodramatic', as he had wanted Callas in his operas for her theatricality.

Visconti directed more operas than films, and more theatre (nearly twice as much) than opera. To him the differences between the media were essentially unimportant: 'Cinema, theatre, opera I would say is always the same kind of work. Despite the enormous diversity of means, the problems in making a spectacle come alive are always the same.' What linked these three means for him was melodrama, 'perhaps the most total form of spectacle'.[6] In that sense cinema, like theatre, was simply a means or a technique for the realisation of a form extrinsic to the cinema.

Much of the discussion of melodrama concentrates on its emotionalism, its tendency towards symbol, its relation to a world in crisis, its extravagance, its moral schematisation, its unreality. Visconti stressed its elements of complete spectacle combining decor, props, costume, music, dance, voice, acting; that is, not the everyday, still less the political or meaningful, but rather the 'experience', the sheer joy of fantasy, colour, light, movement, magic, in short the total liberty of the marvellous and the extraordinary.

Melodrama, for Visconti, was this opportunity for spectacle more than it was anything else, and one of the contrasts in *Rocco*, which is also a contrast in value, is between characters who live melodramatically, who are noticeable because they are colour and movement, and characters who live in an ordinary way, who are very still, very dull, very mediocre, like Ciro. The value of Rosaria, like the value of the melodrama which presents her, is that she 'lives', that she is light, theatre, gesture, sound and thus in her very being goes beyond the everydayness and dispassion of the middling. Rosaria, but also Simone and Rocco, are mythological beings who incarnate all that is exceptional in a world in which almost everything is moderate. It makes of them, even in their vulgarity, aristocrats.

The meaning of the rape, the significance of the murder, the import of Rocco's victory in the ring, the consequences of Rosaria's outburst at the Gianelli's, literally pale before the sensual splendour of the scenes, less about meaning, still less about 'reality', than they are about the qualities of the marvellous that the theatre alone seemed able to deliver for Visconti. The narrative only partially captures such sensuality. Rosaria's performances, the musicality of her voice, the rhythm of her gestures, the languorous acceptance and mockery of death in Nadia's embrace of her killer, the pain in Rocco's eyes, the scent of sex, the body as movement, the weight of objects, go beyond any narrative function to the concrete pleasure of the spectacle, not its sense but the drama of its sounds and coloration. It is at this place that Visconti's cinema is at its most abstract, most pure, most splendid and most powerful, not in the heaviness of social significance, nor in the dire consequences of good and evil, nor in a perverse psychology, but in the ecstatic pleasure of giving birth to fictions.

It is being artistic, theatrical, melodramatic – in short, fictional – that is affirmed in the film as an absolute realm of liberty. Freedom is not in being at one with the world (Ciro), but in being outside it, which is where the film is (in melodrama), and where Rocco is, and from where, in saintliness, he helps to destroy it. Rocco enters the world to fight in its theatres (the boxing ring), resigned to a vulgar necessity, in an attitude of aristocratic disdain, a Prince of Salina however humble in origin.

The great advantage of the move to spectacle, and particularly melodramatic spectacle, is the advantage of play, of turning words into music (the arias and choruses of *Rocco*), of gesture into dance, of objects into light and shadow, or into something as ineffable as density and volume. The murder, the rape, the fight of the brothers are, literally, choreographed, made into an exquisite ballet of murder, or a jazz composition of rape whereby limbs become plastic values and grunts and thuds the sound of music.

Turning to fiction (in whatever form) is a turning to a mode of speaking where ordinary speech fails. Visconti took this tendency towards fictionalisation to an extreme by choosing melodramatic forms in which sound, music, rhythm, counterpoint – all that attests to the inexpressivity of language – are the very stuff of the fiction and where the significances of the fiction reside. The best scenes of *Rocco* are when meaning and words become sound and movement and detail, when sense is shifted by what is outside of sense, which Visconti called melodramatic spectacle and which was the style and the principal content of his films.

The particular forms of his fictions were refuge and protest against a reality from which the exceptional and the marvellous seemed to him to have been lost. The restoration of the marvellous, named by

Visconti as a realm of pure freedom, was a means where reality was transformed and displaced by the variety and richness of artistic forms, notwithstanding political alibis to the contrary.

Ciro, the critic Pio Baldelli commented, was 'correct to oppose himself to the past, though the world which he looks forward to is neither beautiful nor inspiring. ... It is a necessary and just world, but it lacks all magic, all passion. It has never been touched by all-consuming feelings, nor by struggles with the irrational.'[7]

XII

. . . .

In 1948, Visconti staged a production of Shakespeare's *As You Like It*, with sets by Salvador Dali and a cast which included Vittorio Gassmann, Paolo Stoppa (Cecchi in *Rocco*) and Rina Morelli. The play was set not in the seventeenth century ('puritan, austere, rigid'), but in an imaginary eighteenth century ('full of colour, gaiety, melancholy').[8] Visconti chose Dali because he was open to every possibility of the theatrical and the spectacular.

The production was severely criticised, especially by Communist critics who condemned Visconti for departing from reality, for indulging in a decorativeness without meaning, theatrical fantasy without sense. This kind of critique became a constant among a section of Italian critics for most of Visconti's career. For example, Lino Miccichè on the ball scene in *The Leopard*:

> ... a convulsion of fabrics, knickknacks, candelabra magnificently suggesting the very cultivated Viscontian narrative structure, nevertheless confirms at the same time the poverty of energy, the decorative overabundance, the philological character of things under glass that ends by flattening out motivations and characters as in a kind of fascinating and spectacular jewel box.[9]

Visconti replied to his critics in an article in the Communist Party weekly *Rinascità* in December 1948. The article is a justification of 'theatricality', of the freedom of fantasy, not only as a defence of a certain artistic practice but as a protest against a politics of culture which he regarded as reactionary and 'bourgeois' in its demand for harmony, for the suppression of dissonance: 'Must we believe that until the advent of socialism we ought not to play music, or paint, or compose verses?'[10] Visconti objected to left critics' objections that he had turned meaning into spectacle, whereas for him the very meaning of the Shakespeare (and, I would assert, of *Rocco*) was contained in its spectacle:

> ... a musical concerto at the limits of ballet; the characters, in the dialogue and action, are music and dance; the reversals in the story, in their improbability, are variations on a theme of fantasy. In short, we are in the realm of the most complete liberty.
>
> Is it wrong to have made my actors 'leap' too much? This is exactly what I want to do. Until today dramatic actors were tied to the chair, the couch, to the table in the eternally present 'salon'. ... I have made them move, gesticulate, dance. Modern theatre tends towards dance, not in an aesthetic sense, but rather in the sense of 'liberated' movement.

Visconti had scandalised a notion of bourgeois theatre by shifting away from dialogue as the principal bearer of meaning, towards theatrical forms. He made form the very content of his theatre, particularly difficult for critics in search of forms as instruments to frame an ideology. 'Perhaps they think that the theatre exists to repeat endlessly what one reads in the journals or hears at political meetings.

The sense of scandal to bourgeois forms and the demand for liberty in the theatre also informed Visconti's operatic productions. He had revived *melodramma italiano*, a form of lyric opera which was 'dramatic', overblown, hysterical, histrionic – in short, vulgar. And the vulgarity was associated with what was central to Italian popular culture, not simply of the nineteenth century, but of the late 1950s. As Visconti disrupted the habits of the theatre in Italy, he also disrupted its operatic repertoire by scandalising sensibilities of good taste, not only by staging *melodramma italiano*, but by staging it in all its historical veracity, vulgarity, confusion, colour and spectacle.

It is not a criticism of Visconti to call his work 'overblown operatics', as one critic called *Rocco*, or to call it vulgar, exaggerated, artificial, melodramatic, or 'distended, sententious, ostentatiously frank, fundamentally trite, and thematically unsuccessful' (Stanley Kauffman on *Rocco*).[11] Such 'tasteless' effects were precisely the ones aimed for, and those outraged by them were the very people they were meant to outrage. 'This complete ideal ... the melodrama.'[12] There may be a vast range of high culture sources to Visconti's work, and there is his cultivation, his aristocratic and high bourgeois ancestry. But one thing he is not is tasteful or restrained, which accounts for much of the energy of his films.

XIII

The dramatic power of the cross-cutting between Rocco's fight and Simone's murder of Nadia has to do with an earlier accumulation of contrasts and an escalation of intensities between the fights in the ring (on 'stage') and the fights in life (on the street). There are, for example, the two street brawls which spill over from the boxing ring: the riot between supporters of the Parondis and supporters of the Gianellis, and the fight between Rocco and Simone after the rape of Nadia. Fights (on and off 'stage', in the ring/in the street) punctuate the film narratively and rhythmically with theatre as the metaphor of life ('I love melodrama,' Visconti wrote, 'because it is situated precisely at the boundaries of life and of theatre'), an imitation of life, and life the imitation of theatre.[13]

Rocco's sparring with Simone in the gym is echoed by Simone's defeat in the ring, reversed by Simone's battering of Rocco in the Milan streets, reversed again in a further mimicry between theatre and life by Rocco's victory in the ring to 'save' Simone. It is the exact moment in the film when reality and art are directly cross-cut, invading each other's space formally (in a parallel montage), as narratively, and with full dramatic irony, events in reality destroy the purpose of Rocco's victory. The 'sense' of the scene is emotionally conveyed in the reversals, in taking the audience high only in the next moment to fling it low, in the hysteria of the rhythm of the cuts, in the increasing volume of the echoes between scenes, made even more forceful by the screams of the crowd at ringside and the agonised screams of Nadia at dockside.

Overleaf: 'As Simone plunges the knife into Nadia's body, she surrenders to him'

Only opera has ever staged death so grandly or turned life so unashamedly into theatre.

The most artificial, the most theatrical, the most unbelievable, and yet the most compelling and dramatic scene of the film is this death of prolonged writhings and outbursts of pain (the final aria?), where all the intensities of early parallelisms, of bad timing, of 'too late', above all of melodrama and reality, are gathered up, compressed in the final convulsive tremble of Nadia's body.

As Simone plunges his knife into Nadia's body, she surrenders to him, and as they touch each other in an instant of the most intense longing and the most terrible delicious pain, she offers herself to the one she loathes most, and he defiles the one he loves best, a perfectly timed moment of 'too late'. This cross-cutting scene, the dramatic high point of the film, is also its most pathetic. The full impact of the bad timing which has run through the film culminates in the different levels of awareness between characters ('if only' Rocco had known), in the discontinuity between events so that each is the ironic comment on the other, and in the shift in intensity between the comparative paleness of the reality of events in the theatre of the boxing ring and the dramatic richness and import of the theatricality at the flying-boat station as Nadia writhes in the exquisitely rendered pleasures of sadistic pain and masochistic eroticism.

XIV
....

Discrepancy is at the centre of the structure of *Rocco*. The principal discrepancy is temporal, of events or of knowledge coming too late to rescue a life or save a situation or, as in the murder of Nadia, fate overcoming choice, with Nadia destroyed at the precise moment she has chosen her freedom, albeit the freedom of prostitution. It is a similar freedom, similarly discrepant and to no avail, that Rocco chooses in deciding to be a boxer, to sell his body for an illusory freedom, his own and that of the family, destroyed, as Nadia is destroyed, by the passions of Simone. The masochistic pleasure in the erotic pain of Nadia, echoed a scene later in Rocco's writhing on the bed, is the pleasure of the narration which has staged it so deliciously and painstakingly. But for whom?

What is most enjoyable about *Rocco* is the fact that characters act too late, that events are at the wrong time, that actions are inadequate, that Rosaria gesticulates wildly over nothing at all, that actions inevitably fail in their aims. And there is a further inadequacy, perhaps the true source of the pleasure of the film, namely that the predicaments of the characters and the whole range of discrepancies are openly fabricated, made into theatre, so that what is always discrepant is the 'real' situation and the theatrical response to it. The crucial gap is the gap opened by melodrama between an inflated theatricality and over-dramatisation on the one hand (the reason why plot motives often seem so weak in *Rocco*), and on the other hand the actuality and real circumstances to which these relate.

Excess is a term about discrepancy, about means being more than is necessary to meet the needs of a situation. Yet that excess, and the writhings of the characters in their impossible and inadequate responses, are the sources of the film's drama and of its pleasures. There is the masochistic joy for the audience at the writhings, the delight in the inadequacies, the happiness in the awfulness of fate, the ecstasy in the victimisation. This excess and masochistic theatre is not only part of the formal mechanisms of the film (to produce distance, irony, and above all 'gaps'), but is at the centre of its content, since it demonstrates the principal discrepancy between individual lives and historical forces, between personal necessity and social necessity. The emotional force of Rocco, Simone, Rosaria – the enormity of their passion, the depth of their feelings – is no match for the socially and emotionally alienated world which they have entered and which defeats them.

The pleasure in watching them squirm is in proportion to the knowledge the audience has about why they squirm. This too is a function of discrepancy, of knowledge given to the spectator but not to the characters, by means of gaps, bad timing, ironic contrasts, sudden reversals: dramatic discrepancies which make spectator and film-maker complicit in a theatre of melodramatic cruelty as a means to social and political understanding.

Knowledge in Visconti's films is not knowledge in the ordinary sense, because the structures of masochism and suffering which carry them appeal more to structures of feeling than to intellectual comprehension. The appeal is always theatrical, through forms by which a social situation is experienced primarily in emotional terms. What is felt by the characters existentially is experienced by the audience aesthetically, not by words but by sounds, not by concepts but by melodies, not by intellection but by rhymes, not by ideas but by intensities; in short, not by contents but by forms.

It is this formality which expresses, by means of its theatricality, a gap between the demands of the social and the inadequacies of the individual to meet those demands. This is the point at which Visconti's aesthetics become social, and a means of political protest at what reality has made impossible and only theatre is in a position to realise.

Rocco is a story of a social defeat, of what history has rendered impotent. *Rocco* in its form is a triumph of art, the reverse sign of that defeat which, in stating the impossible, is able fictionally to transcend it.

XV

Rocco was released in fifteen Italian cities in October 1960. It grossed Lire 430,904,000 in the 1960–61 season as compared to Lire 768,000,000 for Fellini's *La dolca vita* in the same period, and Lire 732,734,000 for the American *Ben Hur*. Though *Rocco* was by no means unsuccessful in first-release houses, it had nowhere near the success in the large cities that the Fellini film had; yet by the end of 1961, its gross box-office figure was a very considerable Lire 1,527,980,000, earned not in the large cities but on their peripheries and in smaller towns. In the end, it was only second to *La dolce vita* as the most successful Italian film of the season.

The critics did not receive *Rocco* with unanimous enthusiasm (no more than did middle-class audiences), though there was a protest at its failure to receive the 'Golden Lion' at the Venice Film Festival, where it won the Special Jury Prize. But if critics were lukewarm, popular audiences in working-class districts were enthusiastic. It is always difficult to know why a film is popular, but it was probably the melodrama of *Rocco* that appealed to ordinary Italians as it had appalled many critics.

In any case the film made money, and what differentiated it from the naturalism and documentarism of Italian films still heirs to neo-realism, or from the narrative experiments of Fellini or Antonioni, was its attachment to popular categories of good, bad, hate, vendetta, sacrifice, within the popular subjects of boxing and prostitution. These themes had the added connection of the subject of immigration, which was close to the experience of much of the audience (the nine million internal migrants) and within a popular tradition of Italian melodrama which Gramsci had defined as *the* national culture, however much he decried it as exhibitionist, pretentious, dishonest – a national disease.[14]

Italo Calvino, who praised *Rocco* very faintly, and particularly disliked the cultural-literary sources of its narration, its Dostoevskyism, its reliance on Verga, its eulogy to Southern *passionalità*, nevertheless did applaud its theme of migration, of the integration of a rural backward family into the urban metropolis which was the inspiration, he said, of one of the great film traditions, the American gangster film: 'Visconti's film at its best rejoins, deepens and extends the language of images, the rhythm, the light and the bitterness of the urban epic of the gangster film.'[15]

Be that as it may, and even if there was in that tradition and the experience of Southern Italian migration which lay behind it something which touched a popular Italian audience, the apparent sources of the film were the high culture ones which Calvino decried. If the 'moderns' in the Italian cinema seemed to announce the decrepitude of literature (certainly of classical literature), true as much for avant-garde film-makers like Antonioni as for those like Rossellini who were 'documentarists' and 'objective' as if working outside all genres, Visconti's films, to the contrary, seemed to be a reworking and rewriting of classical literary texts. And beyond literature, the reintroduction of an operatic tradition which, however 'popular' in the nineteenth century, had become integrated (with some help from Visconti) into bourgeois high culture of the mid-twentieth century. Verdi, Verga, Mann, Puccini, Dostoevsky were in that sense all of a single piece. The cinema to Visconti was not, it could be argued, the sign of the decrepitude of classical literary culture, but rather the chief instrument for its diffusion.

At first sight the reception of *Rocco* seems very odd. It was rejected by some intellectuals and bourgeois audiences for its literary and operatic aspects, its old-fashioned novelistic techniques and a critical realism which owed something to Tolstoy and Balzac, but it was taken up by socially popular audiences at the urban fringe, as something whose 'truth' genuinely touched them. In one sense, it was an extraordinary accomplishment to have taken the best of bourgeois culture and translated it successfully to the screen, not only for mass diffusion, but particularly to social groups relatively alien to what was then regarded as culture.

The reason *Rocco* was so successful was not that a decrepit and predominantly novelistic literary culture appealed in the provinces or to the Roman working class, but rather that Visconti was able to renew that literary culture in a way more modern than might appear and precisely for the same reasons that he had succeeded in theatre and opera. Visconti did not so much rewrite literature as turn it into a spectacle, and in such a way that one could argue not only that its visceral and sensual forms were its primary content but that this content, so splendid, so rich, so meticulous, indeed so decadent, primarily appealed at an existential level, at levels of involvement, of immediate identification, in short of experience. It was not that *Rocco* was, as many claimed, 'a true film novel', hence full, complex, logical like an old-fashioned narrative tale, but rather that it was a marvellous and breathtaking spectacle, a rich extravaganza in the best tradition of popular film. *Rocco* didn't appeal to the stalls, I believe, for the 'worthy' political-social alibis that were invented for it, but because it was sound, rhythm, melody, tone, colour, volume, intensity, dance, romance, passion: that is, it went to the body, not to the head.

There has been much criticism of the contradictions between the realism of the film and its melodrama, between its politics and its opera, but what matters is not these things but its seductive surface, its garish display, its unabashed excess. Perhaps this is the reason intellectuals found it hard to swallow, not because it was overly literary but because it was hardly literary at all, and instead shamefully, even outrageously theatrical-exhibitionist. Perhaps popular audiences are less concerned than bourgeois intellectuals with decorum and good taste and thus more readily seduced by the things which have always seduced popular audiences: richness, excess, artificiality, all the sumptuous glitter of open fabrication. Perhaps the audiences were a bit like Simone, agog at the lights of Milan from the windows of the tram, seduced by money and sex, dreaming of a night with Nadia at the Grand Hotel at Bellagio for Lire 10, 000.

XVI
....

Vittorio Spinazzola noted that Visconti, from 1956 onwards, possibly as a result of the success of his historical costume film *Senso*, became aware of the commercial value of spectacle.[16] It seemed the precondition for popularity.

Visconti's work appeared to combine two contradictory social-cultural spaces, bourgeois (literature, theatre, opera) and popular (the cinema), with spectacle and melodrama forming the bridge between them. Melodrama was not only, as Visconti said, at the boundaries of life and art, but also at the boundaries of an older elite culture and a 'mass' culture.

Whether or not this is true and however rough the terms (elite/mass), Visconti certainly lent to the cinema the enormous prestige of his bourgeois high culture, while he used popular forms – particularly in the cinema – to make that bourgeois culture not only accessible but relevant, even if so much of his work, including *Rocco*, is record and lament for a culture and values being displaced by modern capitalism. Yet, in that rescuing of an older culture by the instruments of a newer one, Visconti in part contributed to the very disappearance of the things he loved, like the Prince of Salina in *The Leopard*, who used his name and his noble blood to help 'buy' the *arriviste* Angelica and her bourgeois fortune for his nephew Tancredi, a purchase which saved the noble line while corrupting it with contrary values.

Such apparent contradictoriness is posed in *The Leopard*, in *Rocco*, indeed in all of Visconti's films, as inevitable and ineluctable. To preserve the unity of the family in *Rocco*, Rosaria loses it; to capture the love of Nadia, Simone helps destroy her; to save Simone, Rocco utterly ruins him, until all is finished and nothing is left: Rocco has become a boxer he doesn't want to be, the family is fragmented forever, Nadia is dead, Simone is doomed. In this ironic and dramatic split between desires and their impossible realisation, money is crucially important.

Money, in Visconti's films, has an ambiguous role caught between two sets of values, two worlds, even two temporal orders. To save the old in the new society, or more precisely to save what is dignified and human in a world given over to commodities where all values have their price, everyone needs to become a whore, and that, with money as the instrument, is the beginning of the end of things.

None of Visconti's heroes, in *Rocco* or in other films, is concerned with money as such, but rather with preserving something being threatened (the Family, Love, Freedom, Art, Culture) by a new world which they reluctantly need to join (the Parondis come to Milan, Rocco becomes a boxer) and in which money is a necessity to save what is in fact already doomed and their action of salvation sadly only contributes to a further, complete damnation.

Money is a central element in the bad timing, the masochism, the cruelty, the historical disharmonies, the ironies, the discrepancies in *Rocco*: it is the only way to salvation and the surest path to hell. There is no choice, just this awful necessity which seems to issue from necessities of History. The only way to win is not to care about the difference, like Ciro, whom Simone taunts for being a skilled worker at Alfa-Romeo and Rosaria curses as a traitor to the family.

One of the reasons *Rocco* in its structures mirrors the events which those structures form is that the film as popular culture reproduces in its relation to an older culture the very same relation the Parondi family reproduces, and especially Rocco as the aristocrat dressed in peasant clothing. It is interesting that one manner the film studios in Italy used to sell Visconti's films was to sell him as Artist/Decadent, as Star, an extraordinary being, a diva like Maria Callas, a terror like Rosaria and Maddalena, fashionable and a bit corrupt. The image was neither true nor false, but it was an important one to help sell pictures. The popular culture whose values Visconti regretted, and which was undermining the traditional role of the 'artist' which he seemed to embody, was packaging what he stood for as fashionable decadence and turning Visconti the 'artist' into pop star. This was not simply a matter of studio publicity. It was a central, structural feature of Visconti's films: Rocco the Aristocrat was also Rocco the Whore.

XVII

. . . .

Visconti was involved with two ballet productions in the mid-1950s: *Mario e il mago* (1956), based on a Thomas Mann short story which he choreographed, and *Maratona di danza* (1957), for which he wrote the libretto with music by Hans Werner Henze. As early as the late 1940s, Visconti had declared theatre as essentially dance and movement and staged plays accordingly, most notably his productions of Shakespeare, Goldoni and Tennessee Williams. When he began as a stage director for lyric opera in 1954, the same concentration on movement and gesture as dramatic and narrative elements that he had perfected in the theatre seemed even more perfectly suited to the melodramatic forms of opera.

Rocco has no formal dance sequences, but movements are carefully choreographed. They, rather than words, carry the dramatic weight and meaning of the film and the sense of character. Character is expressed more as a kinetic, dynamic quality than as a psychological one, or rather, and more precisely, the psychic inside of characters is translated to the outside, to the glide and sweep of their bodies, to the hesitancies of glances, to the intensity and power of their gestures. Some sequences are very close to dance, especially the fights: the street

The boxers in training: 'less a gym than a ballet class'   Art Center College

brawl after Simone's first victory in the ring (a balletic chorus), the fight between Simone and Rocco after Nadia's rape (a *pas de deux*), and their sparring at the gym (a *pas de deux* with *corps de ballet*) when Rocco is already involved with Nadia, Simone doesn't yet know he has been displaced, and Simone is on the eve of his defeat in the ring and his emotional and physical decline.

The gym in the sequence resembles less a gym than a ballet class, the dancer-boxers on their toes in all their warm-up costumes, tights, gloves, helmets, high-laced shoes, shorts; they sweat, jab, skip, stretch, punch bags, shadow box before mirrors, pose, perspire. The dancing master, Cecchi, encourages some, hectors others, declaims, gesticulates and sings to them, an aria to the dancer-boxers, to Simone of his heaviness, to Rocco of his buoyancy. Cecchi's sight of the beautiful Rocco sparring with Simone brings him out of his office and out of his frustrated rage at the sluggish Simone to 'sing' an aria of the purest joy and astonishment at the feints and jabs of Rocco, his newly found *ballerino*.

Movement and gesture used as dramatic qualities or as the expression of character blur the line between what belongs to themes and what belongs to forms, since thematics are a matter of orchestration apprehended in their rhythms and intensities more than in anything 'spoken'.

There is a crude moralism in *Rocco* which borders on the simplistic – 'good' Rocco/'bad' Simone, 'regressive' Rocco/'progressive' Ciro, but the concrete and externalised realisation of these qualities as primarily aesthetic rather than intellectual is not only what fundamentally creates character and drama in the film, but what gives them all their complexity and power. It is in movement that moods are created and meaning conveyed, and to such an extent that words themselves, and even the progress of the narrative which is moved by structures of reversal, contrast, parallelisms, become 'melodic' or 'chromatic', their primary sense found in elements of form.

XVIII
. . . .

Though the five divisions of *Rocco* have been called 'chapters', it is probably more correct to call them 'acts', not simply because the forms of the film relate more to theatre than to the novel, and a theatre where plastic rather than dialogic and ideological values predominate, but because 'acts' correspond to the five acts of Italian grand opera, the true source of *Rocco*. Prior to these acts there is, as in grand opera, an overture where all the principal themes of the work are set out and, characteristically, in musical and rhythmic form made dramatic.

The 'overture' in the film consists of four distinct movements. The first is slow, majestic, foreboding, the 'destiny' music based on Tchaikovsky played over the credits without any narrative figuration on the screen. The music has two moods, a predominantly dark one punctuated by drums and cymbals and a lighter more lyrical one carried by woodwind as the movement comes to a close. The music dominates the rape and murder scenes, and enters too when Simone first steals (a shirt from the laundry), setting a mood, prefiguring a tragedy, and ironically in something so banal, so harmless as a shirt; it also plays (though with other, contrasting sounds) at the romantic meeting of Nadia and Rocco.

Not only does this musical movement create a mood prior to the narrative, it also establishes itself as a narrative/dramatic content used to underscore action melodically and used too to undercut and counterpoint action, a dramatic element in its own right and a commentative one, like the decor in the film or its lighting.

The second movement, also predominantly musical, continues over the titles, with a slow high-angle shot of a train entering Milan station viewed through iron gratings; the music is a melancholy nostalgic song, 'Paese mio', from the South, but sung in the North, longing for home, for the village that has been left. The main instruments are woodwind and the tone is sentimental, plaintive. A number of contrasts are set, particularly in relation to the preceding movement: voice to instrument, sound to image, cymbals to woodwind, fate to longing, the classical to the popular, the dramatic to the sentimental, high passion to the everyday.

In the first movement music alone carried a dramatic charge; in the second movement, with the addition of voice and of images, the intensity of the opening music is somewhat diminished while visual elements are given a musical function. The relation of song to image is explicitly made in counterpoint.

The music in the second movement is heard again at various points in the film, or is resumed by other songs of longing and sentiment like the 'Non mi avrai' ('I Won't Be Yours') ballad sung by Rocco after Nadia's first entry into the lives of the Parondi family in their basement flat. The one ballad was a longing for home, the other a longing for love which, though sung in a similar harmony, threatens that home. The most forceful and commentative re-entry of the second-movement music is at the close of the film, played with an extra sadness and irony, as Luca disappears in the background of a soulless landscape of newly completed houses. (Vincenzo, the most compromised and conformist of the brothers, is a construction worker and his 'act', which immediately succeeds the 'overture', is about housing, accommodation, resettlement). Luca, by the end of the film, is the single remaining hope of the family that there will be a return to the village in Lucania, and hence some integration between the ancient and the modern, South and North, what has been lost and the 'progress' that has caused that loss. Just before the end, as Luca fades from sight accompanied by the lament of 'Paese mio', from the lost world where the Parondi family had come from so long ago, he caresses with his eyes a seemingly infinite series of posters of Rocco celebrating the bitter victory of social defeat. 'Paese mio' is a ballad of longing, but it is also a concrete structural element, aesthetically felt, of anachronism, discrepancy, ineluctable loss.

The third movement, by far the most narratively important, is without music, or rather the music is composed of natural and inarticulate sounds (shouts, footsteps, train whistles, brushes sweeping down compartments, the clang of chains, uncouplings, the whoosh of steam, mumbles, laughter), of choreographed gestures and actions (crowds sweeping in to greet the train and carry off its passengers, loadings and unloadings, the passing of baskets, stepping down from compartments, pacing to and fro), and of the inconsequential dialogue of arrival of the Parondi family ('We are in Milan' – 'At last' – 'Luca, wake up' – 'Rocco, hand down the basket'). It is not only sounds that are made into music, but also objects and their lighting and shadow, flickering in patterns best described as dense, volumetric and, like the music of gesture and the dance of words, melodic and rhythmic: 'We tried to use lenses and light relations as a musician might ...To make the audience feel the "colours" I used filters and chose a special film stock ... From the very beginning, the shot was violent, dramatic, with a presentiment of things to come' (Giuseppe Rotunno).[17] Just as chromatic variations find their 'emotional' equivalences in sound, or sound finds its equivalence in gesture, these in turn translate into dramatic values.

At the end of the third movement, the family is alone, dwarfed by the immensity of the station. The initial excitement and expectation is replaced by an unease at their sudden vulnerability and the failure of Vincenzo to meet them. The camera pulls away and above them, further isolating them, turning them into things.

The final, fourth movement is accompanied by a jazz piece, quick, light, a bit insipid, played on brass, woodwind and xylophone and associated with the 'city', with lights, glitter, fascination, temptation, speed and a happiness in being part of its colour. As the family climb down the steps of Milan station to find a tram to take them to Vincenzo, in time to the beat of the jazz piece, a new purpose and joy in their speed is there, but so too is their smallness, playthings in a vast immensity, as much mocked by the music as joined by it, miniaturised little dancing dolls.

There is perhaps no better résumé of *Rocco* than this brief overture, which sets out themes as forms, turns music into drama, presents successive moments as analogies, translates linear logic into structural contrasts, establishes a duration only to confound it in a single instant.

In *Rocco* all things become aestheticised, all objects artifice, all reality theatre, all words music, all action dance, all things fabrication, yet not as the contrary to 'life' but rather as its most intense and passionate truth.

XIX

In the script, though not in the film, there is a prologue which is set in Lucania. The brothers bury their father in the sea and with that act turn their backs on the village and their faces toward the North. To leave Lucania for the North was a dream of Rosaria's for twenty-five years. Only the death of her husband now made it possible, a dream to end poverty, to break the bounds of the village, to be somebody, to be called 'Signora'. Her five sons are the instruments of that dream and, as things turn out, the victims of it.

The family 'begins' in the film without the father, though the ritual act of his removal is absent. It is the mother, not the father, who is important to the Visconti family. Visconti's 'family' is a disintegrating social institution within a society whose values and structures are in crisis. In *Rocco*, the disintegration can be ascribed to social causes (the North, the fact of migration, alienated values); but the family is also a psychic institution relating to forces outside the social and perhaps even more destructive: emotions, sentiments, the erotic, the private. Those in the family more aligned with its psychic force, like Rocco and Simone, seem most 'true' and 'real' in the film, whereas those more closely allied to what is social, like Ciro and Vincenzo, seem least true. The social – which is the plainer – is least real (Ciro has lost his soul); the individual – which is more exaggerated – is most real (Rocco retains his soul and suffers).

The correlation in the film between the private, true and psychic and the social, false and alienated makes the family the perfect institution for working out these two sets of values and meanings; but also two sets of styles, and in an apparent reversal, since what is true is represented as the most 'theatrical', whereas what is false is represented as the most 'naturalistic'. This occurs because the socially integrated characters exist only on a surface, whereas the socially unintegrated ones are closer to a psychic depth, to pain, to passion, to emotional forces which are conveyed in the exteriority of their movements, in the rhythm of their gestures – in short, in 'performance', and performance whose particular feature is in reaching great heights and great depths of joy and despair.

Even if Rocco and Simone's characters are less 'social' than the characters of their brothers (boxing is more socially marginalised than construction work or the Alfa Romeo assembly line), nevertheless they are more social, more 'in the world', than their mother is (who is more 'in the family'), and perhaps also more social too than Nadia who, like the mother, is closest to the erotic and sentimental (if only as a dream by the boys) and as a whore is explicitly anti-social (she goes to prison). The performances of these two women ('mother'/'whore') are the most melodramatic and excessively theatrical of all the performances in *Rocco*. It follows from the associations the film establishes that this greater excess is a sign of greater truth, as in the formula: the more theatrical, the more real.

The melodramatic structures with which Visconti works are structures which function to bring into the open repressed truths and hidden realities; it is in such a way that form functions as content. The melodramatic gesture has a substance to it. Rhythm, intensity, melody,

The family: Spiros Focas as Vincenzo, Claudia Cardinale as Ginetta

density are not only aesthetic categories but thematic ones which embody the film and give it a sensuousness. The women, by being more melodramatic, are also closer to the 'formal'; hence the greater performative values of their performances, the more they are 'actresses', splendid, rare, exceptional divas, like Callas.

It is not so much that Rosaria is destructive because she pushes her sons through her overweening ambition (though she does incite Simone to box), or that Nadia is destructive because she pulls them into her arms (the *femme fatale* of popular fiction), as that both bring the boys into touch with areas of the sentimental and the erotic which have a force they can't handle and which, by the very nature of how these areas are structured by Visconti, are anti-social, related not to the public but to the private, not to the historical but to the primal, not to time but to the eternal; hence the greater theatricality of the women, and also their greater mythical quality, the heavenly-damned 'diva'.

If women are more bound in this manner to the instinctual, they are more free of the social, and in so far as the social in Visconti is a realm of the alienated, the greater privacy of women is also a greater liberty and one closest to what is transgressive of the social order. It is to this area of transgression that they bring the men by their actions. Women, at least in *Rocco*, are socially disruptive forces, and however they may destroy men they release in that destruction depths of feeling, which is the place where real liberation in *Rocco* is located. Nadia may have doomed Simone and herself, but those actions, the highpoints of which are marvellous *coups de théâtre*, liberate and bring to the open the very repressive forces which have motivated the actions in the first place. If Simone is destroyed, the audience is made more free, as if it has been taken on a terrible but rewarding psychoanalytic journey which is also a political journey, bringing with it an awareness of the power of social forces.

Theatre is both a means in Visconti's work for the liberation of the repressed and the sign of the repressed, as if repression were what necessitates theatre and fiction as the means to release it. The melodrama of *Rocco* may commit sadistic-masochistic acts for an audience, but it has them face depths to which only such cruelty and eroticism has access and which the exaggerations of the melodrama can perhaps best express.

Visconti's views of the family and of women seem socially retrograde. 'When the family doesn't exist nothing any longer exists. Women can have careers, can be artists, but they need to place the duties of lover, wife, mother above everything else and thus recreate in all its integrity what had been until a century ago the solid structure of the family.'[18] But the fact is that women in his films don't hold the family together, they help to destroy it, not in the name of socially conservative values but in the name of something askew to the social, and more alive, more fundamental, more liberating than the bland social progressivism of characters like Ciro with their insipid fiancées whose kisses are chaste and whose sex is domesticated.

Though Visconti represented women most often as destructive, as in *Rocco*, the representation is neither misogynist nor retrograde: 'I show women in this way if the sense of the narrative and the dramatic construction require it.'[19] Their splendour in his films derives from their belonging to a more passionate and 'human' world; their destructive power is aimed at the social forces that would repress the depths to which they above all have access. This is an ancient depth, removed from the Historical, and it is also the most wonderful, inventive and fictional place in Visconti, the place at which, contrarily perhaps, he is at his most modern.

Visconti's values and the melodramas that issue from them make of him 'the best director of actresses in the world, and [their] performances ...among the most memorable creations of the cinema'.[20]

XX
....

In 1943, just before the fall of fascism, and at about the time of his first feature *Ossessione*, Visconti wrote a now famous essay, 'Cinema antropomorfico', which has been regarded as one of the classic statements of Italian neo-realist cinema in its emphasis on the actuality and humanity of actors independent of any school, any schema, any method. The actor would speak his reality, would express his humanity rather than be subject to the falsity of artifice or evade his reality by means of excessive 'art'.

If the essay is read in relation to his films, particularly works like

Rocco, and in relation to neo-realism, the sense of it seems rather different; or rather it is possible to see in it that feature of Visconti's films, perhaps best realised in the acting, where the attempt to render the real leads to its being rendered theatrically. The 'real' for the neo-realists was there in the surface of reality, and thus it seemed only to require a direct, documentary objectivity to find its truth. In this early essay by Visconti, reality had a human face but one which revealed, in its surface, a depth: the true instincts of the actor, his most intimate self, his temperament, were expressed in terms which veered toward the extravagant.

> My experience has taught me above all that the weight of the human being, his presence, is the only *thing* that truly fills the frame, that it is he who creates the surroundings by his living presence, and that it is his passions which give it movement, give it truth, give it shape; even his momentary absence from the brightness of the frame turns everything back towards its inanimate nature.[21]

'Cinema antropomorfico' is not, as some would have it, an essay about non-professional acting and thus connected to the true-to-life documentarism of some of the neo-realists. It is rather an essay about the central importance of acting, and acting as gestural and balletic, which not only has value in itself but bestows value on objects, on atmosphere, lending them its movement and theatricality and providing them with symbolic meaning defined as a 'giving-things-life'.

Visconti's sentiments are not about objectivity as the means to truth, but about a notion that truth lay in movement, passion, in rhythmic and melodic forms, which could best be expressed, as it is in Visconti, by action and actors whose performances, whose gestures, whose 'animation' are the very soul of his films and which belong, more than to anyone else, to his splendid women: Calamai, Antonelli, Mangano, Magnani, Cardinale, Schneider, and in *Rocco* the nervous, staccato Girardot and the histrionic, melodramatic Paxinou.

XXI

....

There are three homosexual instances or attitudes in *Rocco*. One is from
the point of view of the film and involves an appreciation of male bodies
and their movements: the physical beauty of Rocco, the shyness of
Rocco and Simone gazed at by Morini in the shower, the *corps de ballet* of
boxers in the gym, the grace and the violence of boxing, the dwelling on
flesh and its attractiveness, which though shared by the characters in
their appreciation of each other is primarily a matter of the position of
the camera-narration and its relation to the audience. This is
homosexuality, if not as art, as the subject of an artistic, aestheticising
look in the classical tradition of painterly representations of the male; it
has an odd feel about it in the film, at once tasteful (in its references)
and kitsch (by its setting).

A second position is from within the fiction, and is a view of
homosexuality as corrupt and ugly: it marks Simone's decline as thief,
decadent, male prostitute, and Morini, his client-benefactor, as cruel,
afraid, venal. Homosexuality here is about the disintegration of person,
the slide into barbarism and crime. Simone physically falls apart, loses
fights, shuffles, becomes threadbare, unshaven, shakes, skulks, pleads.
He becomes weak, lost, mean, frightened and he becomes a homosexual
whore. Homosexuality here, like prostitution and like boxing, is linked
to cash and crime; that is, to an alienated and even tragic sexuality
caught up in the values of a modern world where bodies are
commodities, the selling and negotiating of which are a sign of that
world and a subjection to it. Homosexuality becomes something lovely
gone horribly wrong, a decadence.

A third position is directly erotic from within the fiction: love
between men, in this case an ambiguous love of brothers for each other,
Rocco and Simone, adding the crime (?) of incest to the crime (?) of
homosexuality, and in such a way as to combine an erotic and socially
prohibited act (homosexuality) with another of the same kind (incest)
but one linked to the disintegration of the family. This homosexuality is
'pure', part of the sacrifice offered by Rocco for his brother, their
passionate fight and their writhing of love on the bed at Rocco's victory
celebration being the exact duplicate of the ambiguous murder/love-
making of Nadia and Simone as he enters her body again and again

with his knife and she screams and twists in pain.

This more 'pure' and less openly stated homosexuality, even with the overtones of incest which it contains, is connected to a social order in which brotherly love without the calculations of the progressive Ciro and Vincenzo is still possible. Women are interesting in relation to this transgressive, reticent yet 'positive' homosexuality since, if they don't openly provoke it, they are the instruments for bringing men to the edge of it. Nadia, after all, is not simply the source of brotherly enmity, but the direct stimulus to brotherly love. It is she who produces an eroticism in both brothers which causes them each in their way to destroy her: Rocco's rejection of her (for Simone), Simone's degrading and violation of her (directed to Rocco), and finally a murder which both brothers participate in through the instrument of a parallel cross-cutting which places each symbolically in the space of the other; behind Simone's knife is Rocco, both brothers together dealing with an erotic and psychic force that overcomes and destroys them.

XXII
. . . .

Rocco was passed by the censors without cuts for its Venice Film Festival presentation and for its opening the next day on 14 October 1960 at the Capitol Cinema in Milan; it was scheduled to open within a few days in Rome, Catania, Bari, Florence and Trieste. At the Venice screening and the Milan opening, the more violent and sexual scenes were greeted with jeers and whistles by the audience.

On the day after the Milan opening the Attorney General of Milan requested a private screening of the film from Goffredo Lombardo at Titanus and suggested cuts of nearly fifteen minutes to the more 'shocking scenes': the night of love between Nadia and Simone, the rape of Nadia, the fight between the two brothers, the murder of Nadia. Visconti was indignant: 'I won't cut the slightest thing from my film. I don't intend to mutilate my work and I contest the right of the Milan Attorney General to make such a request since *Rocco* has been cleared by the censors ...'[22] He was supported publicly by Lombardo.

The issue was taken up in the press, with the newspapers on the political left being particularly angry at yet one more inroad into artistic freedom by the state and in the name of a provincial, Catholic, conformist morality. The power of the state was revealed in all its stifling conservatism, as if in confirmation of the political-social sense of *Rocco*, where the social order is regarded as repressive of the individual, of fantasy, of passion, of the very sources for Visconti of fiction and the essential subject of fiction.

The issue also opened up a split within state institutions between a relatively liberal censorship and a more conservative judiciary. It was not the first time that *Rocco* had suffered state censorship: the scene of Nadia's murder had to be shifted from the flying-boat station outside Milan to Latina because the Milan authorities refused Visconti permission to shoot something so 'obscene' within the city's boundaries.

The debate went on while the film continued to be screened without cuts. The judiciary, which had initiated the request for cuts in the name of public morality, found itself under attack both by the quality centrist newspapers like Milan's *Corriere della Sera*, and from the left press. The Attorney General of Milan wrote to *Corriere* with a little lesson on art and obscenity in response to an editorial which challenged the judiciary to seize the film if it was indeed obscene. The Attorney General acknowledged that the film was 'art' and for that reason he didn't want to ban it (Art as Sacred); on the other hand it did offend public morality, and he only wished that the authors would take such social responsibility seriously and accede to the recommended cuts.

The Judiciary has never sought to pronounce on the artistic merits of the film, nor is it within its competence to do so. On this count, and authoritatively, the critics have spoken and besides it is sufficient to refer to the prize won by the film at the Venice Film Festival which confers on it the quality of 'work of art'. In any case the Censor has approved it to be screened. If the film had not been recognised as a 'work of art', it would have been deemed in certain places – in the judgment of the Judiciary – as being obscene and in that case being in contravention of some sections of the Criminal Code. No discussion, no deals – because the Judiciary once faced with a criminal violation cannot admit of negotiations of any kind – but only an admonishment. Because if there exists, as there does, a problem of the protection of art, there also exists a problem of the protection of decency. And it is precisely for the protection of what is considered decent that the Attorney General ... wanted to intervene with a sensibility only equalled by his enlightened sense of civic responsibility.[23]

Within two days of this letter and a fortnight after its premiere, screenings of the film had the sections considered obscene by the judiciary blacked out, almost certainly with the agreement of Titanus and Lombardo. A week earlier Lombardo had not only defended Visconti's position not to entertain cuts, but had presumed to speak on behalf of the entire industry when he expressed his fears at the 'artistic' (and doubtless commercial) effects of the judiciary intervening in the composition of films, since whatever may have been the artistic merits of the offending scenes, it was they which, in their spectacle but also in their transgression of 'decency', promised larger than usual returns at the box office. Visconti angrily declared, in the name of artistic freedom, that it was no longer possible to work in Italy and that he would cease to do so from that moment.[24]

Lombardo a few days later agreed to the cuts recommended by the judiciary, which prompted Visconti to express his regret:

As far as I am concerned this is the worst possible solution. You have to tough it out and let the Attorney General seize the film. It is in everyone's interest for the thing to be brought to trial. Otherwise what guarantee do we have in the future? They might black out scenes in the cinema, turn out the lights in the theatre, leave pages of novels blank. If the cuts are accepted, at least let them be projected as black leader so that the public will be aware of it.[25]

By the end of October, not only had Lombardo accepted the cuts, but the Censorship Appeal Board officially decided to reverse the original Board decision and to sanction the cuts asked for by the judiciary.

A year later, Visconti wrote an open letter in the Communist Party newspaper, *L'Unità*, to the Interior Minister, Folchi, who had made it clear that if the matter were solely up to him he would either have banned the film completely or severely cut it – though it was not exactly certain, Visconti noted, how and in what way it would have been 'clerically mutilated'.[26]

Visconti took the opportunity to confirm his faith in democracy and the people, against a state apparatus which was, if not semi-fascist, conservative and repressive in the extreme.

> It confirms in me an already deep conviction that every crumb of liberty which we enjoy in our country is not due to those who govern ... (one asks oneself how they can find themselves in positions of such great responsibility), but to the vigilance, the resistance and the struggle of opposition and of democratic public opinion. If there had not been a substantial protest on behalf of *Rocco e i suoi fratelli* not only by Italian culture, but also by the political parties, the press and the organisations of the left, one can be certain ... that the film would have been denied its constitutional right to make contact with the large mass of spectators and to enjoy, in such a way, the support of the public that all are aware of and that – it is worth noting – has resulted in the greatest box-office returns for an Italian film in some time, after those of *La dolce vita*.[27]

Because of the scenes cut and despite the mutilation of the film, the controversy over the censorship helped the commercial fortunes of *Rocco*, accounting for some of the box-office success Visconti mentioned in his letter to Folchi.

The scenes that the judiciary had wanted censored were scenes of sex and violence. And while there was nothing extraordinary about a censorship centring on these kinds of events as 'obscene' or as an 'outrage to public taste', nevertheless it had a particular point with regard to *Rocco*, since these scenes were violent or erotic precisely because they were intended as points at which the pressure of social repression and all the psychic force it had helped to contain suddenly exploded in socially transgressive – and therefore dramatically extreme and theatrically powerful – acts.

These fictional actions in the film which the Italian state contrived to mutilate and censor as a concrete act of political-social repression were, within the fiction of the film, examples of an equivalent action of repression. Simone's violence and the passions unleashed in the film are given, by means of melodrama, a social understanding, and are a protest against a form of society which has made victims of characters like Simone, Rocco, Nadia, Rosaria. The scenes mutilated by the judicial censors in the name of decency were not scenes of sexual passion, but of the social-psychic victimisation which had provoked such passion and which the judiciary by its actions reduplicated.

If the melodramatic forms of the film mirror the content of what occurs within it – and both have an aspect to them of 'bad timing', of being cultural anachronisms, left behind by time and History – it is precisely the force of such anachronisms, a force Visconti insisted on and attested to, that seemed to so trouble the modern Italian state. And so, in a final irony of bad timing, they cut into the film, seeking to domesticate it, to contain unseemly passions, and by so doing helped to guarantee its commercial good fortune.

The state seemed unable to tolerate the expression of Viscontian melodramatic passion which in part was a protest against its repressive values. It was this state that Ciro inherited and probably in the long run certainly conformed to, Ciro who called the cops and betrayed his brothers, obedient to those 'laws of men' which Rocco explicitly denounced in favour of his 'love' for Simone, a love that was 'immoral', 'illegal', that transgressed all the norms which the progressive Ciro so desperately sought to obey.

It is interesting that the first act of the film, albeit outside its precise fictional boundaries, is the removal of the father, the representative of all Fathers perhaps and hence of the very basis of what is legal and social. His founding absence in the film helps begin a journey through the anti-social which in the end refinds a safe, grey, progressive regime of fathers again, fathers like Ciro who run to the police and even become the police. But until that moment there is all the passion, the rhythm, the extravagance, the drama, the fiction of *Rocco*, outside the ordinary and the legal whose social and symbolic precondition perhaps was that the Father was not present, buried at sea in order that the Parondi family could go North and have its splendid melodramatic adventures, even despite the mutilations which the Law of the State would later bring to them.

XXIII
··························

Italy has been regarded as a land of colour, vivacity, movement, gesture ... and, as Gramsci lamented, melodrama. In a wonderful essay on Stendhal, Roland Barthes mentioned that going to the opera at La Scala in Milan was not simply music and spectacle on stage, but music and spectacle off stage. Everywhere there was a sensuous delight to eye and ear ... and *gelati*.

This '*italianità*', so much a popular image and more often than not created by Northern Europeans and Anglo-Saxon culture and later by Italians as a tourist image, was displaced by another image of '*italianità*', post-war, in Italian neo-realist films. It was a darker, heavier, slower image whose dominant note was less gaiety than a gloom and sadness, an image of difficulty, of hardship even if tempered by a humanism of an ultimate hope, love and progress in the films of De Sica, Neapolitan-flavoured though set in Rome, like *Sciuscià* (1945), *Ladri di biciclette* (1948), and *Umberto D* (1951) and the sombre war trilogy of Rossellini – *Roma, città aperta* (1945), *Paisà* (1946) and *Germania anno zero* (1948). And stylistically, against the excess and histrionics of melodrama these films placed an often dour documentary naturalism, a refusal to stress, to intervene, to point, to comment, quite the opposite to what seems most characteristic of Visconti and certainly of *Rocco*.

Yet – and it is a matter of critical stress and sometimes of critical chagrin – Visconti's work, and *Rocco* in abundance, is excessively realistic and detailed to the point, repeatedly mentioned in this study, of theatricality since the realism seems so meticulous and overwrought. The chagrin is the chagrin at an apparently unresolved contradictoriness between realism and melodrama, between what is objective and historical and what is psychic and hysterical. These doubts and dissatisfactions with Visconti's works, though they take various forms, always come down to this gap between seemingly incompatible styles and sentiments, for example in *Rocco* between a realistic political consciousness represented by the flat Ciro and the melodramatic excess of the more exciting and attractive and strangely 'realistic' theatrical figures of Rocco, Simone, Nadia, Rosaria.

The fact is that the realism in *Rocco* which bears all the weight of history and the social is a realism to be overcome, in the sense that the real is what all persons must encounter as an objective yet psychic obstacle. The weight of the real must be felt in order for the struggle against it equally to be felt. Hence, and despite all the emphasis in this study on the theatricality of *Rocco*, the dance and rhythm of its movements, its melodrama and Italian *vivacità*, in fact the mood of the film is always dark, foreboding, slow and heavy as simultaneously and at considerable length (three hours) the film builds a realism and a melodrama, an objectivity and a psychic distress until they come to their terrible and tragic conclusion, a conclusion akin to an explosion, the bursting forth of pressures which only 'reality' in its repressiveness and obdurate power can have induced.

And just as the 'force' of Rocco's sacrifice and Simone's self-destruction can only be measured against the contrary conformity of Ciro and Vincenzo and the progressist hopes concentrated on Luca, so too can the power and force of the melodrama only make sense measured against the inevitable strength of History, the overwhelming power of the Social of which Rocco and Simone are only apparently the victims and Ciro and Vincenzo only superficially the victors. In the end it is the film which wins. And the price paid for that victory, the very stake of it, is Visconti's passionate splendid realism, which has moved through *Rocco* not as contradiction, but as the very condition of the film's power – and grace.

NOTES

· ·

1 Luchino Visconti, 'Pessimismo dell'intelligenza non della volontà', *Schermi*, no. 28, December 1960, p. 322; in English as 'The Miracle that Gave Man Crumbs', *Films and Filming*, vol. 7 no. 4, January 1961.

2 Guido Aristarco, 'Una storia italiana: Rocco e i suoi fratelli', *Cinema Nuovo*, no. 148, November–December 1960, p. 521.

3 See Gilles Deleuze, *Cinema 2: The Time Image* (Minneapolis: University of Minnesota Press, 1989), pp. 94–7.

4 Luchino Visconti, 'La ragioni di un gusto', *Filmcritica*, no. 76, April–May 1958, p. 85.

5 Ibid.

6 Ibid.

7 Pio Baldelli, *Luchino Visconti* (Milan: Gabriele Mazzotta, 1973), pp. 208–9.

8 Luchino Visconti, 'Sul modo di mettere in scena una commedia di Shakespeare', *Rinascità* vol. V no. 12, December 1948, reprinted in G. Callegari and N. Lodato (eds.), *Leggere Visconti* (Pavia: Amministrazione Provinciale di Pavia, 1975), pp. 28–9.

9 Lino Miccichè, 'L'inafferrabile presente di Luchino Visconti' in L. Miccichè, *Il cinema italiano degli anni 60* (Venice: Marsilio Editori, 1986), pp. 223–4.

10 Op. cit. *Leggere Visconti*.

11 The phrase is quoted by Geoffrey Nowell-Smith in his essay on Visconti in Richard Roud (ed.), *Cinema: A Critical Dictionary* (London: Secker & Warburg, 1980), p. 1047. Stanley Kauffman, 'Some Accidents of Truth', *New Republic*, vol. 145 no. 1, 3 July 1961, p. 32.

12 Luchino Visconti, 'La mia carriera teatrale', *L'Europeo*, nos. 13–14, 1966, reprinted in *Leggere Visconti*, p. 63.

13 Luchino Visconti, 'La ragioni di un gusto', p. 85.

14 Antonio Gramsci, 'Il gusto melodrammatico', in Gramsci, *Letteratura e vita nazionale* (Rome: Editori Riuniti, 1987), pp. 80–3.

15 Italo Calvino, 'Quattro domande sul cinema italiano', *Cinema Nuovo*, no. 149, January–February 1961, p. 33.

16 Vittorio Spinazzola, 'Rocco e i suoi fratelli', in Mario Sperenzi (ed.), *L'opera di Luchino Visconti: Atti del convegno di studi Fiesole 27–29 giugno 1966* (Fiesole: 1966), p. 310.

17 Requoted in André Cornand, 'Rocco et ses frères', *La Revue du Cinéma/Image et Son*, no. 244, 1970, p. 138.

18 Quoted in Ernesto G. Laura, 'Il linguaggio nei film di Visconti', in *L'opera di Luchino Visconti*, p. 98.

19 Ibid.

20 Andrew Sarris, 'Luchino Visconti's Legacy', *Village Voice*, 15 January 1979, p. 37.

21 Luchino Visconti, 'Cinema antropomorfico', *Cinema*, nos. 173–4, 25 September–25 October 1943, pp. 108–9.

22 Guido Gerosa, 'L'odissea censoria', *Schermi*, no. 28, December 1960.

23 Ibid.

24 Ibid.

25 Ibid.

26 Luchino Visconti, 'Lettera al ministro su "Rocco e i suoi fratelli"', *L'Unità*, 24 October 1961.

27 Ibid.

CREDITS

· ·

Rocco and His Brothers
(Rocco e i suoi fratelli/Rocco et ses frères)

Italy/France
1960
Première
6 September 1960 at Venice
Film Festival
UK trade show
13 September 1961
Production company
Titanus/Les Films Marceau
Producer
Goffredo Lombardo
Production manager
Giuseppe Bordogni
Production supervisors
Anna Davini, Luigi
Ceccarelli
Production secretaries
Romolo Germano, Mario
Licari
Director
Luchino Visconti
Assistant director
Rinaldo Ricci
Second assistant director
Lucio Orlandini, Jerry Macc
Script
Luchino Visconti, Suso
Cecchi D'Amico, Pasquale
Festa Campanile, Massimo
Franciosa, Enrico Medioli
Story by
Luchino Visconti, Vasco
Pratolini, Suso Cecchi
D'Amico, based on the book
*I segreti di Milano: Il ponte
della Ghisolfa* by Giovanni
Testori
Dialogue
Luchino Visconti, Claude
Brulé
Script supervisor
Albino Cocco
**Photography (black and
white)**
Giuseppe Rotunno

Camera operators
Nino Cristiani, Silvano
Ippoliti, Franco Delli Colli
**Assistant camera
operator**
Roberto Gengarell
**Second assistant
operators**
Osvaldo Massimi, Enrico
Fontana
Music
Nino Rota
Musical director
Franco Ferrara
Songs
'Paese mio' by Nino Rota,
Giagni, performance by Elio
Mauro; 'E vero' by/
performed by Umberto
Bindi; 'Tintarella di luna' by
Migliacci, De Filippi; 'Il
mare' by Pugliese, Vian
Editor
Mario Serandrei
**Art direction and set
decoration**
Mario Garbuglia
Assistant art director
Ferdinando Giovannoni
Assistant set director
Pasquale Romano
Costumes
Piero Tosi
Wardrobe
Bice Brichetto
Make-up
Giuseppe Banchelli
Hairstyles
Vasco Reggiani
Sound
Giovanni Rossi
Stills
Paul Ronald
180 minutes
16,200 feet

Alain Delon
Rocco Parondi
Renato Salvatori
Simone Parondi
Annie Girardot
Nadia
Katina Paxinou
Rosaria Parondi
Roger Hanin
Duilio Morini
Paolo Stoppa
Cecchi
Suzy Delair
Luisa
Claudia Cardinale
Ginetta Giannelli
Spiros Focas
Vincenzo Parondi
Rocco Vidolazzi
Luca Parondi
Corrado Pani
Ivo
Max Cartier
Ciro Parondi
Alessandra Panaro
Franca, Ciro's fiancée
Adriana Asti
Giannina, laundry worker
Claudia Mori
Laundry worker
Nino Castelnuovo
Nino Rossi, Simone's friend
Franca Valeri
Widow
Rosario Borelli
Billiard marker
Renato Terra Caizzi
Alfredo, Ginetta's brother
Eduardo Passarelli
Sauveur Chioca
Emilio Rinaldi
Bruno Fortilli
Rocco Mazzola
Gino Seretti
Felice Musazzi
Luigi Basagaluppi
Becker Masoero
Franca Valeri

BIBLIOGRAPHY

....

The most extensive writings, and the best on Visconti generally and on *Rocco and His Brothers* in particular, are in Italian, and there are some fine essays in French. Writings in English are less abundant and less good, in part perhaps because of an aversion in Anglo-Saxon culture to the particular mix in Visconti's work of operatic melodrama and political commitment. Nevertheless there are some excellent studies of Visconti in English.

Though written some time ago, Geoffrey Nowell-Smith's *Visconti* (London: Secker & Warburg/BFI, 1967) is still the best study in English of the films; it contains a chapter on *Rocco*. In 1980, Nowell-Smith contributed the Visconti entry in Richard Roud (ed.), *Cinema: A Critical Dictionary* (London: Secker & Warburg, 1980); the essay is more critical and less appreciative of Visconti than in Nowell-Smith's book but it is dense and comprehensive.

There is a splendid essay by Thomas Elsaesser: 'Luchino Visconti', *Brighton Film Review*, no. 17, February 1970; it ought to be read with his general essay on film melodrama which, though centring on the American cinema, has insights which are interesting for Viscontian

melodrama: Thomas Elsaesser, 'Tales of Sound and Fury: Observations on the Family Melodrama', *Monogram*, no. 4, 1972, pp. 2–15.

There are two general works on opera and melodrama which I found useful for understanding *Rocco*: Herbert Lindenberger, *Opera: The Extravagant Art* (Ithaca: Cornell University Press, 1984), and Peter Brooks, *The Melodramatic Imagination* (New Haven: Yale University Press, 1976).

There are some interesting insights into Visconti in Andrew Sarris's brief reflection on Visconti's career, 'Luchino Visconti's Legacy', *Village Voice*, 15 January 1979, p. 37. The few pages (pp. 94–7) in Gilles Deleuze, *Cinema 2* (Minneapolis: University of Minnesota Press, 1989), are incisive and stimulating.

On *Rocco* in particular, it is probably worth mentioning Roger Manvell, 'Rocco and His Brothers', *Films and Filming*, October 1961; Derek Prouse, 'Rocco and His Brothers', *Sight and Sound*, Winter 1960–61; the *Monthly Film Bulletin* review, no. 334, 1961, p. 153, signed 'R.V.' [Robert Vas]; various statements by John Gillett and others in *Film*, no. 27, January–February 1961, pp. 12–13; and Peter Armitage's essay, 'Visconti and Rocco',

in *Film*, no. 29, Summer 1961.

In English, translated from the Italian and specifically to do with *Rocco*, are: Luchino Visconti, 'The Miracle that Gave Man Crumbs', *Films and Filming*, vol. 7 no. 4, January 1961, and in the same issue, Guido Aristarco, 'The Earth Still Trembles'.

In French, translated from the Italian, there is a very interesting article by Goffredo Fofi, 'Le sud dans le cinéma italien', *Image et Son*, no. 195, June 1966. There is an important interview by Jean Slavik, 'Rencontre avec Visconti', in *Cahiers du Cinéma*, no. 106, 1960, and another interview in *Cahiers*, no. 93, March 1959, by Jacques Doniol-Valcroze and Jean Domarchi. Also worth mentioning in French are: François Weyergans, 'L'ancien et le nouveau', *Cahiers du Cinéma*, no. 119, May 1961; Yves Guillaume, *Visconti* (Paris: Editions Universitaires, 1966); Robert Benayoun, 'Pour un bilan positif du sujet', *Positif*, no. 40, June 1961; André Cornand, 'Rocco et ses frères' *La Revue du Cinéma/ Image et Son*, no. 244, 1970; Pierre Bourdin, 'Rocco et ses frères', *Téléciné*, no. 97, June–July 1961; Marcel Martin, 'Visconti et l'histoire', *Cinéma 63*, no. 79, September–October 1963.

By far the best thing I have read on Visconti in French is a brief review of Visconti's production of Goldoni's *La Lacondiera* at the Festival of Paris in 1956, written by Roland Barthes in *Théâtre Populaire*, no. 20, 1 September 1956, pp. 70–2.

As I said, most of the material is in Italian. What follows is a brief list of works I found of particular interest.

Guido Aristarco and Luchino Visconti, 'Ciro e i suoi fratelli', *Cinema Nuovo*, no. 147, 1960.

Pio Baldelli, *Luchino Visconti* (Milan: Gabriele Mazzotta, 1973).

Alessandro Bencivenni, *Luchino Visconti* (Florence: Il Castoro Cinema, 1982).

Giuliana Callegari and Nuccio Lodato (eds.), *Leggere Visconti* (Pavia: Amministrazione di Pavia, 1975).

Ermanno Comuzio, 'Musiche e suoni nei film di Visconti', *Cineforum*, no. 26, June 1963.

Renzo D'Andrea, 'Le musiche di Rota da Visconti a Fellini', *Cinema Nuovo*, vol. 30 no. 274, December 1981.

Adelio Ferrero (ed.), *Visconti: il cinema* (Modena: Comune di Modena, 1977).

Ugo Finetti, 'Il tema della famiglia nell'opera di Visconti', *Cinema Nuovo*, no. 202, November–December 1969.

Lino Micciché, 'L'inafferrabile presente di Luchino Visconti', in Micciché, *Il cinema italiano degli anni '60* (Venice: Marsilio Editori, 1986).

Mario Sperenzi (ed.), *L'opera di Luchino Visconti: Atti del convegno di studi Fiesole 27–29 giugno 1966.* (Fiesole: 1969).

Luchino Visconti, 'Cinema antropomorfico', *Cinema*, nos. 173–4, 25 September–25 October 1943, pp. 108–9.

Luchino Visconti, 'Pessimismo dell'intelligenza non della volontà', *Schermi*, no. 28, 1960. There is an interview in the same issue entitled 'Rocco un profeta disarmato'.

Luchino Visconti, 'Lettera al ministro su "Rocco e i suoi fratelli"', *L'Unità*, 24 October 1961.

It is worth noting a number of responses (the respondents included Italo Calvino, Galvano della Volpe and Franco Fortini) to a questionnaire sent out by *Cinema Nuovo* concerning *Rocco*, published as 'Quattro domande sul cinema italiano' in nos. 149–51 of the journal between January and June 1961.

The script for the film was published by Capelli Editore: Rome in 1978, edited by Guido Aristarco and G. Carancini. It contains a lengthy essay by Aristarco, 'Esperienza culturale ed esperienza originale in Luchino Visconti'.

. . . .

The print of *Rocco and His Brothers* in the National Film Archive was acquired specially from Intrafilms, Rome.